Alice
   You are a blessing.

   love
   Ann Makena.

Parenting Children
into
Wholeness

Strong, Lifelong Relationships with Your
Children and Maximized Potential

ANN B. MAKENA

WESTBOW
PRESS°
A DIVISION OF THOMAS NELSON
& ZONDERVAN

This book is a work of non-fiction. Unless otherwise noted, the author and the publisher make no explicit guarantees as to the accuracy of the information contained in this book and in some cases, names of people and places have been altered to protect their privacy.

Scripture quotations marked NKJV are taken from the New King James Version. Copyright 1982 by Thomas Nelson, Inc. Used by permission. All rights reserved.

Scripture quotations marked NASB are taken from the New American Standard Bible, Copyright 1960, 1962, 1963, 1968, 1971, 1972, 1973, 1975, 1977, 1995 byThe Lockman Foundation. Used by permission.

Scripture quotations marked NIV are taken from the Holy Bible, New International Version. NIV. Copyright 1973, 1978, 1984 by International Bible Society. Used by permission of Zondervan. All rights reserved.

Unless otherwise indicated, all scripture quotations are from The Holy Bible, English Standard Version (ESV). Copyright 2001 by Crossway Bibles, a division of Good News Publishers. Used by permission. All rights reserved.

WestBow Press books may be ordered through booksellers or by contacting:

WestBow Press
A Division of Thomas Nelson & Zondervan
1663 Liberty Drive
Bloomington, IN 47403
www.westbowpress.com
1 (866) 928-1240

Because of the dynamic nature of the Internet, any web addresses or links contained in this book may have changed since publication and may no longer be valid. The views expressed in this work are solely those of the author and do not necessarily reflect the views of the publisher, and the publisher hereby disclaims any responsibility for them.

Any people depicted in stock imagery provided by Thinkstock are models, and such images are being used for illustrative purposes only. Certain stock imagery © Thinkstock.

ISBN: 978-1-9736-0509-6 (sc)
ISBN: 978-1-9736-0508-9 (e)

Library of Congress Control Number: 2017914973

Print information available on the last page.

WestBow Press rev. date: 11/3/2017

DEDICATION

Dear God, the thought of you as my Father takes my breath away. Your character makes it clear what a parent should be like. Your love and sacrifice are unconditional. I have learned to trust you more with each passing day. I am in awe of you, Father. I am blessed to be your child. To my children, Sally and Nate, my prayer is that I am the best mother I can be for you, my lovely delight from God. My father, Joseph, and mother, Dorothy, you are my heroes. You are such wise parents. Because you didn't write a parenting book, I write this book in your honor.

CONTENTS

Preface xi

Acknowledgments xiii

Introduction xv

Part 1: Things to Keep in Mind 1

There Is No Perfect Parent 1

Parenting Is about Your Child's Life 2

Dealing With Guilt 3

Your Wholeness Matters 4

A Few Years of Your Impact Will Last Your Children
Their Lifetimes 5

Parent Child Relationship Lasts a Lifetime 5

Bitterness in Later Years 6

Maximizing your child's potential 8

Things versus People 10

Raising a Talented Child—The Foundation
Matters Greatly 11

What Is the Human Foundation? 12

Instead of isolating, insulate your children 13

Parental Blessings 14

Unity among Parents/Adults in the Home 16

Adult Family Dynamics and Relationships 17

Conflict resolution 18

Maintain self-respect with your children 19

Children Cope with Life as Well as Their Parents.............20

The Earlier, the Better..20

Keep It Age- and Gender-Appropriate................................21

When Change Is Needed..22

Loss and grief..23

Part 2: General Parenting—All Parents 26

Pray for Your Children...27

Intentional Foresight (Have a Vision)..................................28

Quantity and Quality of Time...29

Start from Day One... 31

Demonstrate Love and Affection 32

Why Unconditional Love? 32

Faith 34

Nurture Uniqueness..35

Priority...36

Communication...37

Commitment...39

Being Intentional 40

Discipline...41

Discipline during Parenting 42

Decision-Making...44

Hard Work/Work Smart..44

Boundaries..46

Consistency..47

Stability 48

Being vs Doing 49

Teach Them Gratitude...50

Self-Education 51

Let Children Be Children 52

Be Patient 53

Train Your Children to Read 54

Advocating for Your Children 55

Nutrition 56

Healthy Touch 56
Be Intentional about Your Spiritual Home Environment 57
Being Aware of the Subconscious Mind 58
In Case of Adoption 59
During Separation or Divorce of Parents 60
Children in Abusive Homes 62

Part 3: Single Parenting **66**
Acceptance 67
Let God Cleanse Your Heart 67
Take Individual Responsibility 68
Help Children Understand They Are Not to Blame for
the Circumstances 69
Help Build Their Self-Worth 70
Keep Your Emotions in Check 71
Self-Care 72
Realize You Can't Make Up for the Missing Parent 72
Set Standards for Your Life and Your Children 73
Develop Your Faith 74
When Finances Are Tight 75
Get Educated on the Missing Pieces 75
More Sacrifices and Harder Work 76
Shun Away Shame 77
Strong Boundaries 77
Teach Children Respect for the Other Parent 78

Part 4: Advanced Parenting **81**
Acceptance of the Situation 82
Giving Up Control 83
Self-Care 84
Your marriage 85
All Our Children 85
Raising Our Child with Advanced Needs 86
Spiritual Development 87

Nurturing Emotional Development 88
Raising a Victor in Your child 89
Your Other Children/The Siblings of the Child with
Advanced Needs 93
As the Parent/Guardian Caregiver 94
Having an Inner Awareness Is Helpful 95
Self-Educating 96
A Practice of Spiritual Alertness 97
Engaging in Spiritual Warfare 98
Developing Resilience 98
Develop in Discernment 99
Learn to Encourage Yourself 100
Forgiving Is Necessary 102
Being Okay with Personal Boundaries 103
Family and Other Important Relationships................ 103
Moments of Solitude... 104
Exercise, Nutrition, and General Health 104
Journaling... 105
Decide Never to Quit 105

Part 5: Conclusion 107

About the Author 111

PREFACE

Parenting is a commonly used term. The question is, how often do we seriously think about what good parenting means? Is it only about having children? What makes parenting successful? How do we define success? What about all relationships involved? Is commitment to parenting necessary, and what does that mean? Whose responsibility is it to parent our children, and what does that mean? Are our children the best that they can be? How do we influence their potential as parents?

This book inspires parents and those involved in raising children to take charge and make the best of their children as well as develop life long lasting relationships. Raising children is a lot of work and it is well worth it. The period for making an impact is very short compared to the rest of our children's life. Having a strategy for your parenting and sticking to it makes the whole difference.

ACKNOWLEDGMENTS

I am thankful to God for making me His child and for being my Father and the greatest parent I know. I am grateful He is in my life. His unconditional love has sustained me through my life, and His grace has been sufficient in times of need. It is because of His grace that I get to share the things I have learnt along the journey in various ways about parenting. I am in awe of God.

Thank you, Steve, my husband, and my friend. Your love and support has helped me be increasingly who God has called me to be. I thank you for your understanding through putting together my writing and bringing them to completion. I love you and appreciate who you are. I thank God for my children, Nate, and Sally. We have been through a lot together, and they have remained trusting of the process. I couldn't ask for better children to be mine and to raise. I love you both, and I am thankful for the assignment God gave me when He placed you into my life to be your mother. I take you both very seriously. I am thankful for my parents Joseph and Dorothy for the good work they did in raising us and the sacrifices they made for us their children. Thank you for your advice on life issues. I am thankful for the support they continue to give us in our adult lives. We are so blessed to have loving, dedicated, amazing parents like you pray for God's blessings and sustaining grace upon you. We love you. I am thankful for my siblings Lucy, Mary, Isabella and Koome for always being there and supporting in through my life journey.

Your support has meant a lot in pursuing my life dreams. I wouldn't be me without my family.

Thank you, Pastor Jim Anderson, for taking your time to review this book while in process. God, bless you. Thank you, Dr. Katherine Nickels, for encouraging me to write on advanced parenting and for taking your time to review this book while in process. Thank you, Dr. Breningstall Galen, for taking your time to review this book while in progress. Thank you for encouraging me. Thank you Dr. Michael Zachariello for reviewing this book while it was in process. Thank you, Dr. Anna Milz for reviewing this book while in progress and for your support. I pray blessings on each one of you.

Thank you to Westbow press for editing and publishing this book. Blessings to all those who were involved in the production of this book and Westbow press at large.

INTRODUCTION

Train up a child in the way he should go, and
when he is old he will not depart from it.
—Proverbs 22:6 (NKJV)

While there is no perfect parent in existence, most parents can do a better job or improve on a good job if they put more thought into it. Parenting is a challenging undertaking, and this book is meant to encourage parents to do the best they can. Each child is extremely unique, requiring unique care and understanding. This book does not give details for every situation but acts as a guide to various subjects on raising a whole child.

This book has five major sections:

1. Some things to keep in mind. A parent-child relationship is a lifelong relationship. Oftentimes, we tend to focus on what seems to be getting us by now and don't take time to think about what that might mean down the road.
2. The second section is general panting strategies that any parent can apply to building up their children into wholeness. This can help them deal with whatever life brings from a place of strength.

3. The third section addresses issues related to single parenting and what may help make the best of the situation.
4. The fourth section addresses issues related to advanced parenting, including raising a child with a chronic medical condition or any abnormality, and what might help in making the best of the situation.
5. The final section is the conclusion.

Having studied, observed, and applied a lot of what I share, I am confident in sharing with others and believe others can experience positive results with the application of what I share. Getting information alone does not transform things. It's the application of the information that makes the difference. If what you are doing is not working, try something new.

EXPRESSION OF FAITHFULNESS

Look at the sun
As she makes her way
Through the beautiful skies
Her rays smiling gloriously
Are seen by all, alike
Her warmth like a blanket
Felt equally alike

Look at the sun
Rising in the morning
Always from the east
Never from the north
She strolls across the sky
Gently like a dove
Seen by all alike

Look at the sun
Setting in the evening
The colors that surround
As beautiful as can be
She vanishes shyly
As though she is aware
Of millions eyes watching

Look at the sun
Never changing her course
Trustworthy to lead the way
Dependable to brighten all
Consistent in everything
In her life, we find
True expression of faithfulness

by Ann Makena

PART 1

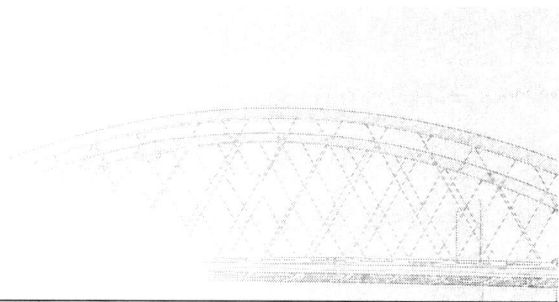

Things to Keep in Mind

There Is No Perfect Parent

Many good parents carry the burden of shame and guilt over mistakes that have happened or something that didn't turn out as expected. In hindsight, it is very easy to see things we could have done differently. Destroying yourself with guilt and shame doesn't make up for what went wrong. No matter how good a parent we work at being and how many parenting books we read, there may still be things we won't know how to handle. At some point or another, we still will make mistakes, and some things may not turn out as expected. Because there isn't a perfect human being and there aren't perfect circumstances in this life, it is impossible to be a perfect parent. This book is meant to inspire parents, grandparents, and others involved in raising a child to make the best of what is available. It is meant to support parents in the process of making necessary changes to get better results out of impacting the lives of your children. We all can make our lives better, and equally, we can improve our parenting skills.

It is easy to wish we could go back and do some things differently. And while we can't undo the past, we can do something about now to make a difference in the future. Our focus should be on what we can do, starting today, to improve the results we hope for moving forward. No matter what stage we are at in the parenting journey, we can improve. If things didn't start right, we can make positive changes. The only thing we should never expect is to be a perfect parent. Instead, we do our best and stay gracious to ourselves because sometimes things will go wrong. If God gives us grace, we need to grow into receiving that grace, as well as giving it. When you beat yourself up, you are simply taking away energy that you could use helping your family. Acknowledge when things aren't right, learn from it, work toward a better tomorrow, and show your love. Forgive others by loving and forgiving yourself.

Parenting Is about Your Child's Life

Our number one reason for having children and raising them is so that they can grow up and have their own lives. Having children is one of the most selfless things we can ever do on earth, and it never turns out well when done for selfish reasons. Our children are here to fulfill a purpose that is put in them by God. They are not here to fulfill our needs, even though it feels good to have them. There is nothing wrong with enjoying our children or how wonderful they make us feel as long as that does not become the primary reason in our actions while raising them. Our main goal should always be to support them and help them figure out their purposes. Their lives are separate from ours as parents, and we must prepare to release them wholeheartedly when the time comes, which is one of the hardest things to do.

Our children are not meant to be our friends while we are raising them. It is important to keep checking whether what we are doing is for the good of the child or because it feels good to us. For example, if we give our child candy because it makes them happy, and we enjoy seeing them happy, is the candy for the good of the child or because the results feel good to you? Our focus on what's best for our children will keep us disciplined in our choices and actions for them.

Some parents unconsciously use their children to fulfill them. Instead of focusing on what the child needs, they get what they need out from the child. For example, when a lonely parent manipulates a vulnerable child to fill that gap of loneliness. In such cases, some parents might guilt their children into not having friends or use blackmail to cause distance between their children and their friends as a way to keep the children to themselves. It can be as simple as watching a movie together or going shopping. The parent gains companionship at the expense of the child. This type of parent/child relationship is unhealthy. While these types of parents hope, things will never change because they are getting emotional support and companionship through the children, the children will most likely end up resenting the parents. Many of these children are unable to maintain a relationship with their parents once they grow up and attain their independence, which then leaves the parents resentful, and the cycle continues. Parents must seek friendship from an equal adult and maintain a selfless parent/child relationship with their children while raising them. When children are raised selflessly, they grow up to be selfless and are in a better positon to give back, not only to their parents but the community at large.

Dealing With Guilt

Due to our human imperfections, guilt is bound to show up from time to time concerning how we parent our children like any other area of life. We need to keep in mind the hind sight bias. Sometimes, we make mistakes due to the information we have at the time. Later, we might realize we were wrong but it's too late. Instead of letting guilt rule, we can admit we were wrong and then take appropriate steps to correct the situation. Nothing is hopeless until we give up. Living with guilt is a waste of time. It is like walking on a trend mill to go grocery shopping. It keeps your mind busy but does not accomplish the results you want. Prayer is one way of getting rid of guilt. Other ways can be talking to someone about your situation and how you feel. You may find out that you are not the only one making such a mistake. You may also find out you didn't really do anything wrong but need to get information to help you deal with the new things as your children continue to develop. Keeping ourselves educated over time also helps us avoid some mistakes and find ways to correct those we already made. Keep in mind that no parent is perfect including you. Give yourself grace and you will be able to give others grace.

Your Wholeness Matters

A person can only give what he or she has. You cannot raise a child into wholeness before you become whole. It is important to take time to know who you are as a parent and become secure in being you. Who you are makes a greater impact on your children than any teaching you will ever give them. Your children will most likely copy you before they do the things you tell them they should do. Therefore, once you become whole, you demonstrate wholeness without having to talk much about wholeness. How you handle life is how your children learn to handle life. For example, if you are a person who use curse words whenever you get frustrated, your children will see that as the normal thing to do and use the same language. You cannot train your children something you don't live by or at are least working on.

Wholeness also keeps your energy focused where it needs to be. Living in brokenness takes too much of your energy. Brokenness often causes us to make wrong choices, as well as be in wrong relationships and wrong places, which can cause more hurt to not only the parent but to their children. Inner healing and direction makes life easier, which, in turn, makes us better people and parents. You may read more about wholeness in my book *Become Whole, Unbreakable, and Unstoppable.*

A Few Years of Your Impact Will Last Your Children Their Lifetimes

Generally, a parent has about eighteen years to instill values in their children that will take them the remaining of their seventy or so years. It is therefore important to pay attention to how we want to see our children handle their lives when they become adults and aren't depending on us for their life decisions. Raising children with foresight can help them make better judgment calls between what feels good now and causes pain later and what is uncomfortable now but will bring joy later in life. It is easy to overlook many needed aspects of parenting if we are focused on day-to-day activities and what makes us all happy to get through each passing day. Time goes very fast, and once we lose the time we have while our children are growing, we cannot recover it. Sometimes we postpone parenting for other things only to realize those things cannot buy back the time that's been lost. For example, we can get caught up building our careers, thinking we will be more involved with our children once the career is stable only to realize our children found other relationships and it's too late. We can build our lives once our children are grown, but we can't buy back our children once we lose them.

Parent Child Relationship Lasts a Lifetime

Every parent's desire is to have a good, lifelong relationship with their children. Raising your children only lasts for approximately eighteen to twenty-five years. However, the relationship (good or bad) that develops during those few years lasts the rest of your lives. Many parents end up not having a relationship with their children as they get older, which is sad for both the children and parent. The truth is that how we raise our children has a lot to do with the relationship they have with us once they are grown up

5

and independent. The question is, why do so many parents lose the relationships they have with their adult children?

Parenting is challenging in many ways. It takes time, energy, and resources, which makes it easy to focus on just getting by each day. However, the result of not paying attention to full life while parenting can be devastating overall, including relationships with adult children in our old age.

Bitterness in Later Years

Sue (which is a fake name), was a woman who lived in a nursing home after she couldn't take care of herself at home any longer. Almost every time I saw her, she was groaning bitterly with tears running down her face. As weeks turned into months, I noticed that many physical changes began to take place. At the beginning of her life in this facility, she sat up straight in her chair when she wasn't crying and her hands were functioning. She could pick up her spoon and feed herself, as well as do whatever she could while in her wheelchair. When she began to cry, she could fold herself tight and make a tight fist as she cried bitterly. Oftentimes, I engaged her in attempt to comfort her, but she was very difficult to comfort. When she spoke to me between her tears, she talked about her children. She was bitter that they let her go to the nursing home instead of caring for her at home. She talked about the fact that they did not come to visit her at the nursing home. She said bitterly many things about her children and sacrifices she had made for them while raising them with her husband who had died before her. Yet, they did not show any care for her now that she was old. Each time I spoke to her, Sue clenched her teeth and bitterly repeated the stories of her children.

As months passed by, she cried increasingly, including about the fact that no one stopped to listen to her sorrows. She was left alone unless someone was giving her care. I also noticed that her physical body was changing. She became permanently bent over, and her fists became permanently folded. She lost the use of her hands completely and developed severe pain due to being so contracted. It was extremely sad to watch Sue live the last years of her life this way, and by the time she died, she couldn't speak anymore but instead gnashed her teeth as she groaned and cried bitterly. I often wondered what the other side of the story was. Why did her children not come to see her in the nursing home or show any concern even though she had raised them and sacrificed for them? I did not get to hear the other side of this story.

However, during years of working as a chaplain, I came across many other older parents who were in similar situations as Sue. In their old age, their adult children didn't show any care or concern for them. And I knew many others who had bad relationships or no relationships at all. As a professional, most elderly people I worked with seemed sweet, and I was left wondering why many adult children were minimally or not at all involved in their older parents' lives. In the cases where the parents poured out their hearts, they shared a lot of sadness and talked about how much they missed their children. They thought about them and wished they could see them, as well as their grandchildren, but they didn't. In old age, many of the older family members and friends had died, leaving life to be increasingly lonely with each passing day. This made them long for their children even more.

The adult children I talked to shared how difficult it was to relate to their parents because they didn't have a relationship growing up. The father was never home because he worked away from home or was too busy with his own life while the children were growing up. The mother was too busy with at her job and with other commitments and missed her children as they grew. Most of these people learned to seek relationship elsewhere and left their homes of origin as soon as they could. Most parents are still at an age that they are busy when their children grow to be adults and move on to start their lives. Most of these relationships are left unattended or neglected until the parents are old and looking back to where they left their children. The sad part is that many people don't realize they never really had a relationship with their children until it's too late.

No matter how bad your situation has been, anyone can turn things around at any time. Young parents can start to raise their children intentionally to develop strong relationships at a young age. Parents of teenagers who didn't start right away can change things by having a conversation about what went wrong and how it can be corrected. Older parents whose children are adults can have a conversation with their adult children about what went wrong and how they can work things out before it is too late. The good thing is that even though it might be a little late for some, it can help shape life for your children and your children's children.

Maximizing your child's potential

Doing who we are is the greatest and most fulfilling way to live our lives. Instead, many of us become what we do which is why we don't find true fulfillment. For example, when you ask many people who they are, they tell you what their job title is (what they do), instead of simply telling you their name. What are the things that come automatically to us? What are the things we dream about and think about in the quietness of our lives? What are the things that excite our hearts even when we think they are beyond our reach? What is the one thing or so that comes so easy to you and keeps surfacing in your heart over and over even when you are trying to forget about it? As a dad or a mom, have you maximized your potential? Are you fulfilled? Is there more you could do with your life and how does that make you feel?

Discovering your purpose and working towards living it brings great joy and fulfillment. You enjoy doing it, you find time to do it and you don't necessarily do it for money. Once you discover your purpose, passion come alongside which makes it a priority in your life. Hard work is required but may not be felt because joy counters it. Our purpose comes from God and He is a rewarder of those who diligently seek Him. This is the very reason we make our children's life better by training them to develop their purpose, talents, and gifts.

It is one thing to raise great children who don't get in trouble but it is another thing to raise children who pursue their life purpose and maximize their potential. Raising good children may give them a good life but training them to maximize their potential gives them fulfillment. We have a lot more potential than we utilize within our lifetime which is unfortunate. We are trained to go for our needs which mostly means get a job and pay our bills. Many scientist, artists, doctors, great teachers etc. live and die without ever fulfilling their purpose. A lot of creativity in us go to waste. One question we should ask ourselves is; what would we truly want to do if all our bills were payed? With our children, we can start to pay attention to their true passions while they are young and nature those passions. If they love to write, take them to writing classes and provide them all materials to encourage them write. Listen to their imagination with interest and encourage them to imagine more. If they like drawing, singing, or helping those who are suffering, support those passions any way you can. It is not a waste of time. Instead of encouraging our children to focus on a major that will bring them more money which is all good, it is better to discover who your child is and nature who they really are and what their purpose is. The fact is, we may not see where our child's passion is leading them to because they might be the one to come up with something that no one else did.

As we raise our children to be great citizens, we should also be intentional about helping them live their best and most fulfilled life which comes with realizing their purpose and living it. A well-rounded child is a child who grows knowing how to navigate life without getting in trouble and is living their purpose and is fulfilled at heart.

Things versus People

One of the major complaints I heard from elder parents was, "All my children want from me is my things or my money. They don't care about me."

Often, this doesn't start overnight or when the children are all grown. It usually starts while parents are raising the children, and it starts with the parents, because a parent trains a child in the way they should go whether consciously or unconsciously. The more parents give gifts to make up for lost time or whatever other guilt they are dealing with, the more they are training their children to relate to them in that very manner. How a child is raised does not change just because a parent is old and the child is now an adult. God created human beings as social beings; therefore, what is natural to humans is relationships. Anything that takes the place of relationships isn't natural and causes destruction to relationships instead of building them.

Many parents spend a lot of time away from their children either at working, school, or other activities. These are all things that need to be done, and the more things parents put on their plates, the more time is taken away from the children. Many of these parents also carry the guilt of being absent from their children, so they find ways to make it up to their children, whom they dearly love and don't want to hurt. They buy big things or take them on expensive vacations once or twice a year. During these vacations, kids play and go on rides and have fun, and by the time they get back home, everyone is exhausted but must return to work or school. No time for relationships is left or given a thought. The saddest part of this is that the children don't care how much money their parents spend. Although some parents talk with their children about the expense of vacation, but all that makes absolutely no sense to a child.

The fact is children need their parents and a relationship with them, not things. When a child's life is filled with things instead of the presence of a parent, that child learns to expect things instead of the parent's presence. However, most parents are too busy to realize this until they are old and lonely. Then why are parents surprised later in life when their children don't have a relationship with them?

Instead of working long hours to give your children things and take them on expensive trips, work enough to live as reasonably as it makes sense for you and purpose to spend time with your children while they are growing. Don't work for a paycheck and pay day care to have a relationship with your children if there is something you can do differently. Fight for that relationship; get to know your children, and let your children get to know you. When you get old, then your children will most likely be beside you whether you have money to give them or not.

Raising a Talented Child—The Foundation Matters Greatly

> Therefore, whoever hears these sayings of Mine, and does them, I will liken him to a wise man who built his house on the rock: and the rain descended, the floods came, and the winds blew and beat on that house; and it did not fall, for it was founded on the rock. "But everyone who hears these sayings of Mine, and does not do them, will be like a foolish man who built his house on the sand: and the rain descended, the floods came, and the winds blew and beat on that house; and it fell. And great was its fall. (Matthew 7:24–27 NKJV)

All our children are talented in one way or another, but we must admit there are children who are exceptionally talented. No matter what the level of talent, a foundation is extremely important in raising a child. Having no foundation leaves our children vulnerable to all storms of life. Having a weak or a cracked foundation holds for a time but eventually caves in. Think of a builder. The first thing that happens is he goes downward, deep into the ground. The bigger the building, the deeper and wider the foundation they dig and build. We can't build a twenty-story building on a two-story building foundation. It will not hold up. If we are building a two-story building with hopes to expand later, we must build the dream foundation to hold the dream when it flourishes. Have you ever wondered why some very successful people in life end up committing suicide for lack of satisfaction or whatever else? We would expect very successful people to hold it together, but it is not always the case. A foundation is key in every person's life.

Secondly, the bigger the building, the greater the loss. A two-story building is visible to those around. But a fifty-story building is visible to many more from a distance. Many are known to the community we live in, but others are known to the whole nation. For example, a president is known to nations, while a nurse may be known to the community in which he or she lives and serves. If something goes wrong, the grief over the nurse comes from the community, and the grief over the president comes from the nation. The foundation of a gifted and talented child must be well thought out and intentional to hold them through the rough storms of life.

What Is the Human Foundation?

This is who we are. Our identity is more important than wealth and fame even though all have their place depending on how well used. The identity of a person is the solid ground the person stands on. When we don't get deep into who we really are, we are driven and tossed around by any racing wind no matter how old we are. Our identity is not based on the things we do or acquire. A talented child brings excitement to the parents. We must not focus on the talent and forget who the child is. Talking about the talent always and showing great excitement all the time makes a child identify with the talent instead of who he or she is. We need to be intentional about promoting virtues like gratitude, humility of heart, kindness, sensitivity to others, and hard work. While it is okay to celebrate talent or intelligence, we must be intentional to build who he child is. Love the child for who he or she is. Don't fall in love with the talent. Instead of always telling a child how smart or talented he or she is, talk about how hard working and kind that child is. Help the child attach success to effort and promote values more than talent. When children grow up with a deep sense of identity and values, they can overcome life's challenges, but when we develop talent without a foundation, it seems great on outside but the person is not fulfilled on inside which causes them life challenges.

As Christian believers, our identity is in God through Jesus and God's word is our solid rock. Giving our children a strong foundation of His word keeps them solid throughout their lives. We need to train them that the gifts and talents are from God and for God's glory and help them understand to please God in all they do. A strong identity in God cannot be shaken no matter what life brings.

Instead of isolating, insulate your children

Protecting our children is one our responsibilities as parents. Many times, we can be tempted to keep our children as far away from danger as possible. Isolation is keeping away from something to protect. Isolating our children from what we perceive as a danger to them helps in some occasions and most times temporarily. Looking at the world around us, we don't need to go far to find trouble. Trouble is in our neighborhoods, schools, churches etc. It is nearly impossible to hide from the things we don't like and the things we hope our children can keep away from. The best way to prepare your children for life is to insulate them. This means to put a coat around them that protects them no matter what is around them. For example, if an electric wire is not insulated, it must be isolated to avoid short circuits and related accidents. However, an electric wire that is insulated does not need to be isolated. No matter where you place it, it is safe. In the same way, it is important to insulate our children with the right believes and values that will carry them through life without chasing after isolating them from everything. Train them the reverence of God in all their ways and they will be able to stand against the environments you are afraid of. There are many other things included in insulating your children which include everything in this book and more ways you come up with. The right values, giving them security, love and discipline, showing them they matter to you by making them a priority, among others.

Parental Blessings

As believers, God is our Father, and our greatest blessing comes from Him. I start with that statement because our earthly relationships can be complicated at times. God our Father has given everyone His blessing and looks forward to seeing everyone receive it. Therefore, people don't need to feel like they have no one to turn to during various situations. However, as much as is possible, our goal should be to receive everything God has in store for us, including that of our earthly relationships. God, from the beginning of law, ordained a certain order for all our relationships. The relationship between child and parent is special because it has a promise attached to it in the commandments.

In the book of Genesis 49 is the story of Jacob giving his blessings to his twelve sons before his death. His son Joseph had favor with his father, and he received great blessing. His words to all his children were intentional because he gathered them for that purpose before he died. "All these *are* the twelve tribes of Israel, and this *is* what their father spoke to them. And he blessed them; he blessed each one per his own blessing" (Genesis 49:28 NKJV). In Genesis 27, Jacob receives a blessing from his father. It was so important to him that he deceived his father to get the blessing. Parental blessings are very important to a child's life. God ordained it to be, and leaving it out of our lives causes us and our children to miss an important aspect of life.

Among God's original commandments, He tells us how a child should relate to parents. "Honor your father and mother, that your days may be prolonged in the land which the Lord your God gives you" (Exodus 20:12 NKJV). Examples of other scriptures that speak to child-parent relationship include the following:

"Children, obey our parents in everything, for this pleases the Lord. Fathers, do not embitter your children, of they will become discouraged" (Colossians 20:20–21 NIV).

"Children, obey your parents in the Lord, for this is right. Honor your father and mother-which is the first commandment with a promise-so that it may go well with you and that you may enjoy long life on earth" (Ephesians 6:1–3 NIV).

A child is not born knowing what this means and a parent is responsible for training their children what it means because nothing else we do can change what God has commanded.

Proverbs 1:8–9 (NKJV) says: "Hear, my son, your father's instruction, and forsake not your mother's teaching, for they are a graceful garland for your head and pendants for your neck."

When raising your children, it is important to train them the importance of blessings. Your children are watching how you relate to your parents and the older people around you. Parental blessing is biblical. As a parent, it is important to raise your children in such a way that you line them up for your blessings as well as the blessings of others around them. If you raise your children in a good environment and give them your unconditional love, most probably your relationship will be good, which sets the environment up for blessings instead of bitterness and curses. How you treat your parents and other older people around your children makes a big difference how they will treat you when you are old. The first commandment with a promise attached to it by God is: "Honor your father and your mother, that your days may be long upon the land which the LORD your God is giving you" (Exodus 20:12). The Bible also warns fathers not to provoke their children but to raise then in the ways of the Lord. Some parents wait until their children are grown up without training them right to start preaching the scripture to them. This usually doesn't go very well. The most effective way to have line up your children for blessings is to train them the best you can while they are growing up by providing a balanced intentional parenting including love, discipline, boundaries etc. and always overseeing your home as a parent. If your children learn to respect you and your authority at a young age, they will respect you at your old age and respect other authority in their lives which will cause them to the blessed wherever they go.

Unity among Parents/Adults in the Home

The adults in the home could be a husband and wife or other family settings like aa single who lives with their parent, grandparents, or maybe an uncle and aunt, etc. Children have their own minds. Many times, they believe they know what they want or what is best for them, but they need your guidance as they grow and learn to make their own decisions. Young children growing up and teenagers need help, support, and guidance. Often, parents or other adults in the home underestimate children, but children are smart and quick to figure out how the adults in their lives operate. Children can be great at playing the adults in their lives to get their way. Not because they are bad children but because they are human and humans naturally go after their interests. For example, a child may want to drink soda or eat cookies right before lunch in a home where this is not allowed. Children are quick to know the parent who is good at boundaries, so they often ask the other parent for permission. Sometimes if one says no, they sneak quietly to the other and ask again as if it is the first time they are asking anyone. In homes that lack unity and consistency, children fall through the cracks in discipline. Secondly, the parents/adults can start to resent each other or have conflict when one is constantly giving in to the children's demands even when it is not in best interest of the children. It is rarely the intent of the children to cause conflict between their parents. For married parents, keep in mind you are always modeling to your children how they should relate to their spouse when they grow up.

Another situation that adults need to pay attention to is lack of wholeness in one or both parents and other adults involved. Some parents seek to fulfill their emotional needs through their children, which causes an unhealthy relationship with the children. In some cases, parents who may feel unloved become consumed with trying to win the love of their children without thinking how they are affecting the children. Parents intentionally need to seek their wholeness for both their sake and the sake of their children, as well as other relationships in their lives. The more people seek to be whole from inside out, the better unity and focus they have to do what is best for everyone involved.

In cases where unity is lacking, having a conversation about it can be helpful. The conversation between adults should be kept between adults and done before things get explosive. When parents and adults in the home are on the same page regarding how the children are raised, it takes away confusion and makes clear what expectations are on the children. Building discipline in children becomes easier, there is more security, and trust is built, which results in better relationships in the home between children and parent and among the adults.

Adult Family Dynamics and Relationships

How the adults within the family relate to each other makes a difference in the development of the children in the home. This does not mean performing for the children but genuine relationships. It is important for adults including husband and wife, grandparents, uncles, and aunties etc., to cultivate healthy relationships for themselves. Good relationships create healthy environments for children to grow in and toxic relationships create toxic environments. We are spiritual beings and children are affected by toxic environment no matter how well we act in front of them. We train our children to be genuine by being genuine and we train them to relate well in their relationships by relating well to each other. Constants arguments, use of bad and demeaning language, gossip, and ugly competitions affects adult's health and affect children at a worse degree. Being intentional about all your relationships does make a great difference overall.

Conflict resolution

All human beings are different and complex which make conflict inevitable in any given relationship. Having conflict is not necessarily a bad thing. It can foster positive challenge and growth if handled well. As adults, we need to deal with conflict positively and help our children deal with conflict positively. Fights, name calling, putting down etc. are negative and immature ways of handling conflict and it affects all family members negatively. The key thing is not to be conflict free because that it impossible. What is important is to accept conflict as part of being different which is a good thing, as part of life and developing positive ways to embrace each other's differences as well as agreeing to disagree some of the times. In times when we wrong each other, we can resolve conflict in humility instead of letting pride get in the way.

When your children are having conflict, never take sides as a parent. It worsens their conflict and could lead to enmity. Instead, let them resolve their conflict unless it is getting out of control. If you get involved, point out what each could have done differently and remind them how important they are to each other. Be intentional about using language that foster the growth of their relationship and validate who they are. Don't put one down in front of the other even when they are wrong. Always build your children up. Talk about what is wrong one on one at a separate time to whoever is on the wrong and differentiate what is wrong from who they are. Reassure them of your love in spite of the mistake because your love should never be based their performance but on who they are.

Discourage one child taking the role of disciplining another child. Remind your children that they are all children and you are the parent and will handle the correcting and the disciplining. Do not join a child who is against the other even if they are on the right. No child should feel overpowered by the other child/ren along with a parent.

Maintain self-respect with your children

Healthy boundaries are a big part of maintaining respect in any relationship especially between you and your children. Your children need you to be their parent and any other way of relating to them has great potential of becoming counter-productive. Boundaries state what lines should not be crossed between relationships. They help guide and protect relationships. Another helpful tip is to practice processing things in your mind before acting or reacting towards your children. Once your children lose respect towards you as a parent, it makes parenting more complicated than it already is. For example, don't get into arguments with your children. It is possible with intention, self-education, and mental practice. Arguments in a home many times start from childhood and becomes the norm but not helpful. As a parent, we can learn to be composed and avoid getting our emotions caught up in our children's behavior. Practice being calm in all situations and don't take it personally when children act a certain way. Once you focus on yourself, you lose the battle because once your children know they can manipulate your emotions they can take advantage of that. Practice to separate yourself from children behaviors and learn to deal with things from outside the circle, not within the circle. Once you start to get hurt feelings from your child and start acting from your feelings, you entered the circle. Staying outside the circle means your actions towards your children are not controlled by emotions but by mental process with allows you to think through and see beyond the behavior which is a symptom of something deeper most of the time.

Children Cope with Life as Well as Their Parents

Our attitudes and choices make a big impact on how our children learn to deal with life. Many times, things go wrong in various ways, and how we handle misfortunes teaches our children how they should handle them. If the tendency of the parent is to fall apart whenever something goes wrong, the children learn to fall apart when things go wrong in their own lives. When parents live in humility and gratitude when things go well, the children learn to do the same. When parents maintain a calm attitude in tough times and don't give up, children learn to do the same in their lives. In cases of sickness, death, or divorce, the parent raising the child has great influence on how the child receives big changes. When parents become bitter and constantly speak negativity at home, children learn from that, and it ends up affecting their lives negatively. How we receive a child with medical conditions or other forms of disability makes a difference how that child receives and is received in life. Because life is unfair, it is the responsibility of a parent to be prepared to demonstrate a positive attitude in life in both good and bad circumstances for their sake and the children's sake.

The Earlier, the Better

It is easier to straighten a seedling than to straighten a grown crooked tree.

Intentional parenting brings great results for your children and makes parenting easier in many senses. As soon as a child is born, he or she is ready for parenting. The early years of childhood are the most critical in their emotional development, starting with the first two years. When the child is seven years old, his or her personality is formed, and takes more work to bring change, although things are never hopeless. The older the child become, the harder it becomes to shape him or her differently. Think of a seedling growing into a tree. It easier to shape it into any direction while it is still young and flexible. Once it starts to toughen, shaping it becomes difficult and it becomes more likely that you will break it in the process. It costs more to get the technique and equipment you need to straighten a grown tree that is crooked. The same applies to our children, which is why we need to start and stay committed sooner rather than later. Taking the appropriate steps to raise young children makes it easier to raise them when they become teenagers and makes relationships better and more trusting when they become adults.

Keep It Age- and Gender-Appropriate

Every child is unique and goes through life's milestones uniquely. However, there are general developmental expectations of each age group and gender. It helps to read each year what children of your child's age are expected to be doing developmentally, behaviorally, socially, etc. The more you read, the more accurate the picture you have will be, which helps in determining how your child is doing. Staying educated can guide you in determining if your child need help, what is normal, and how to handle some of the complicated parenting dilemmas that every parent experiences. Sometimes, you might hear a parent telling a ten-year-old to stop behaving like a baby when the child is really behaving like a ten-year-old. We want to imagine our children are growing quickly and maturing, but they are children growing at their own pace, and we need to be educated so we are better equipped to guide them.

Another very important aspect to keep in mind is that boys and girls develop differently. It would be unreasonable to have the same expectation of them about everything. Reading about raising different genders helps better equip a parent to deal with the differences that exist. Sometimes, our children get upset at each other because they don't understand each other. Parents who educate themselves are equipped to help them understand and accept each other's differences, which builds the relationships between them, as well as the parent.

When Change Is Needed

Sometimes things don't go as we hope they would. Some parents reach a point in life when they come to terms with a need for some changes in their children and their parenting. It is never too late to make changes. However, parents must keep in mind that children may resist change, and it might be difficult and challenging to make changes. That should not keep us from pursuing a positive change. Following are some steps that may make it easier bring about the desired change.

1. Start by prayerfully identifying the change you want to make. We can't make a change if we are not clear on what it is and how positively it will affect us and our children. For example, we may not have appropriate boundaries and realize that it is causing problems in how we relate with our children. We need to be clear about what is happening and be clear that change would make life better for everyone.

2. Commit to it by deciding that you will stay with it however difficult it gets. This is because our children have their own minds, and if the change seems like it will be hard on them,

there will be resistance. We can't back off when faced with resistance.

3. Put together a plan on how you want to implement the change. The more consistence you are with implementing change, the less confusing it will be for the children.

4. Start by communicating with the children. Have a dialogue about the change to help them understand why it is needed. Listen to them and how they feel about it. You may not get resistance right away, because sometimes it takes experiencing the change for the children to feel the effects. Keep your guard up, because resistance may come later. Communicate when the change begins—the sooner, the better.

5. Make appropriate time for the children while going through the change. Keep open and honest communication going. While you show support for how they feel, remain firm about the change and keep reminding them how it will eventually benefit them. With consistency, the new change will become normal. You may visit later to see how the children are doing and what their attitude is toward the change. Using the example of better boundaries, the children may experience feelings of more trust and safety when they can depend on their parents instead of having an equal relationship with parents.

Loss and grief

Death is part of our lives as much as living is. It is important to expose our children to what it means to die, be sick and have pain in life at a young age. Not by inflicting pain on our children but by showing them the reality of pain within family and extended family as well as the world around you. This gives you the opportunities to educate your children how to deal with grief and loss in their own lives. Keep your children hidden from the reality of live will make it difficult for them to deal with same realities in their lives when they will be faced with them, which is normal. We can expose our children by attending funerals of loved ones and friends together, visiting our family and friends in the hospitals, volunteering in a nursing facility or senior living facility and other ways that bring comfort to those in need around us. Many times, how we train our children to deal with grief is how they will deal with us. For example, some adult children will not go to support their dying mother because they want to remember memories of their happy mother. The question that baffle my mind is whether my mother stops being my mother when she is in pain and most probably needs me presence the most. To help our children accept all aspects of life as normal it helps to expose them to all aspects of life at a young age and train them to deal appropriately with life instead of always viewing life from our perspective only. Train your children to have compassion for others who are dealing with death and other types of loss or sickness. If you don't have a tough situation in your family, step out and support those others around you. Many people are shocked when their children refuse to visit them in the nursing home or in the hospital but some of these children have only known what we would humanly call a perfect life and don't know how to handle difficult situations. Death is part of life, wrinkles are part of advancing in age, old age, disability sickness and all difficult things of life will happen to us somehow at some time or another. It is best to train our children to deal with all aspects of life so that they don't fall apart when these things come upon them.

THE CYCLE OF LIFE

While we live, it is given we will die
For some, too soon, for some later
But for sure sooner or later
It is painful, it is inevitable, it is death
It is cruel, has no friend and never invited
Live your best each day while you live
For sooner or later, that day will come
Love with all your heart and let them know
Hold your chidren as long as you can
Show respect to your parents and elders
Support your brothers, sisters and friends
Quit complaining and practice gratitude
Each day you live is a gift to be shared
For sooner or later, that day will come
True love is never lost, not even to death
It is hidden securely in our hearts forever
Choose memories you make with loved ones
Forgive a lot, give a lot, hold your peace
There is nothing you can give after death
So pour yourself out while you live
For sooner or later that day will come

By Ann Makena

General Parenting— All Parents

Train up a child in the way he should go, and
when he is old he will not depart from it.
—Proverbs 22:6 (NKJV)

A ll parents have a limited time to raise their children. What
we do with that time will make an impact on our children's
lives, whether that be positively or negatively. All parents want to be
the best parents they can be for their children. Not all parents end
up having success stories of their children, which can be painful.
The good news is that parenting is not hopeless. There are certain
things we can do to increase our chances of having success stories,
including maintaining close, healthy relationships, which is every
parent's dream. Below are things to think about and practice that
will support your desired dreams in parenting.

Pray for Your Children

God is the master planner, and He designed all of us and our children. He designs each person with a purpose to fulfill. Because he knows our children better than we do, it would do our children and us justice to seek Him concerning our children. Ask Him for wisdom in raising each one of your children per His design and will. Each child is different and has unique gifts. The greatest gift we can give to our children is consistent prayers. Pray for them before they are born, after they are born, and throughout their lives.

Life is filled with warfare. The enemy is running around looking for who to devour, including our children. Life is full of temptations. We never know what our children are experiencing when at school and other places. We need to consistently battle for them in the spirit. When we are in prayer, the Holy Spirit reveals things to us that we may otherwise view as normal or coincidences. He shows us how to listen to our children and truly hear them and how to speak to them so they can hear us.

Pray for their faith in God to increase as they grow older and for them to be grounded in who they are in God. Pray for your relationship with your children to be ordered by the Lord and for them to be fulfilled inside so that they are not vulnerable to seek fulfillment with the wrong company. Pray that they stand strong against ungodly influences even when they are mocked for it. Pray that God would do the inside job in them while He guides you to fulfill your role as a parent in bringing glory to Him. Keep your vision for your children's lives before God always.

Pray for their future. Because God has a plan for each one of them, pray that it is revealed to your child. Pray that there is provision and protection. Pray for their spouses, their children, and whatever else God leads you to pray concerning. Keeping God at the center of our parenting will make everything else flow much better than trying to do it in our own knowledge and strength.

Intentional Foresight (Have a Vision)

"Then the LORD answered me and said: 'Write the vision. And make *it* plain on tablets, That he may run who reads it. For the vision *is* yet for an appointed time; But at the end it will speak, and it will not lie. Though it tarries, wait for it; Because it will surely come, It will not tarry" (Habakkuk 2:2–3 NKJV).

Seeing your newborn baby as an adult and how you desire them to turn out is like having a vision for a business project you plan to work on. For example, when you want to build a house, you start with a mental picture of the house you want to build. You then draw it on a piece of paper and calculate the cost. You come up with a plan on how to bring the home in your mind to reality. As the builders start to build the house, we keep that picture in place and check things every step of the way to make sure the house is coming together correctly. As soon as something goes wrong, it is corrected so that it does not mess up things once the house is complete. Likewise, we need to have a mental picture of our babies as adults. Not as doctors, lawyers, or singers, because that is not up to you as a parent to decide. We need to have a vison of our babies as a kind, gentle, loving, productive, strong adults by the time we are done raising them.

We need to keep that vision at the forefront of our minds and compare our daily parenting to make sure the child is coming up right. We need to make corrections along the way just like the builders do. No parent dreams of seeing a child in jail when he or she grows up—or doing drugs or keeping the wrong company. Not even those who have experienced these difficulties themselves want to see their children walk the same path. Parents want the best for their children, both as children and as adults. This is what we must keep in mind every day of the parenting journey. When we forget this, we are letting the very children we love dearly struggle much more than we realize when they grow up.

For example, we can ignore a negative behavior in a child because we don't want to hurt that child's feeling. The child might hit other kids, and as a parent, we the child instead of correcting the behavior.

(It could be disobedience, laziness, or other behaviors we ignore). As time goes, other parents won't want their children playing with this child. How do you suppose this affects the child? The problem can become much bigger if not addressed. Even though the child is hitting other children, the child doesn't understand why no one wants to play. So, the child internalizes it negatively, and one thing leads to another. Before we know, we have unconsciously destroyed the very child that we were trying to protect. This child can grow up with the same attitude and thus mess up their entire life. Only because as a parent, we focus on today and not hurting their feelings. Instead, we end up hurting their lives.

A big problem we have is that we mostly do what must be done to get through the day and to the next. We enjoy seeing our children happy, and we only want to do what makes them happy, which, in turn, makes us happy. Other times, we get too busy with our own lives, and the last thing we want to deal with is a crying child or to see the child we spend only thirty minutes with each day sad. Basically, we parent by emotions. Unfortunately, this way of parenting usually causes problems for children as they grow up.

The Bible tells us to train our children in the way they should go, and they will not depart from it when grown. Training is different from teaching in that teaching is theory and training is both theory and practical. In training, a person practices an activity until he or she gains that skill. That is what God expects us to do with our children in all areas of their lives. Our fear of hurting our children's feelings as we raise them could immensely hurt their future lives. Intentionally keeping foresight in mind guides our daily decision-making in the process of parenting our children the right way.

Quantity and Quality of Time

Time is extremely important in everything we do. We must invest time into our children to get the best results from parenting.

Having a child does not necessarily equate to knowing that child. To know people, including our children, we must spend both quantity and quality time with them on a regular basis. Spending a few minutes in the evening tired after a long work day every day doesn't give us enough time with our children, even though we refuse to face it.

Lack of adequate time with our children causes many problems. For example, if the only time you spend with your children is thirty minutes before they go to bed every day, the last thing you want to do is spend those precious minutes disciplining them. Many parents who have tight schedules end up giving in to their children's demands to keep them happy, which ends up destroying the children in the end, as well as compromising the relationship between the parent and child. As parents, we must keep in mind that it might work to manipulate children when they are young, but it gets harder as they get older, and that's when problems begin. Conflict become more prominent between parents and children as they continue to grow separately, despite being in the same home. Creating plenty of time around our children makes it possible to grow together as the children age. It gives space for love and discipline without feeling guilty. It makes children feel they matter to their parents, which increases their confidence. Overall, plenty of time helps create healthy relationships when the time is used appropriately.

Quality time means your attention is intentionally on your child. It is possible to spend a lot of time together but not in a quality way. For example, when all day is spent watching television, the focus is not on the child or the relationship. The way people get close is by spending time focused on one another. As parents, it is our responsibility to get involved in activities that foster healthy development for our children, such as reading to/with them, coloring, walking, or going to the park. Paying attention to our children and what is important to them helps them bond with us better. It also helps them grow to be generous and selfless because we train them by demonstration.

Start from Day One

Once children are born, learning begins immediately. They instantly scream at the change of environment. They realize something major has happened, and they respond to their new environment. The mistake some parents make is to wait for their children to grow older to train them. The sad news is that by the time the parents are getting ready to start training their children, the children have learned a lot on their own and from others.

The fact that babies are not able to be understood easily does not mean they are not learning. In fact, the first two years of a child's life is very pivotal emotionally and developmentally. During this time of great vulnerability, the child learns to relate to the world, which carries on through to adulthood. If the parents are attentive and caring, the child learns to trust, and if the immediate care is hostile an unreliable, the child loses trust and develops coping mechanisms that affects other relationship as the child grows and interacts with the rest of the world.

At an early age, children are moldable if parents are intentional and take time to shape them. Discipline, boundaries, language, etc. should start immediately, and consistence makes things easier as the child grows. If a parent lets a child have whatever he or she wants and then suddenly says no at age two, temper tantrum will follow. Many parents are surprised by this and don't like the fight, so they continue give in for the sake of peace. As a result, things only get worse, because children are smart and know how to take charge when adults around them don't know how.

The next important years of develop continue up to age seven. What children learn at their earliest becomes more solid. During the ages when children start to talk, they are very talkative and demanding. It is important to keep in mind that the child is still developing, and how parents respond to them affects their development positively or negatively. Children can be manipulative, and parents who are not intentional can easily lose parenting battles.

The more intentional we are during these early years, the easier it is as they grow older and pass these years.

Demonstrate Love and Affection

Love is a gift and should never need to be earned. Our children should be secure in our love and be clear that they will never have to work to earn it because it is already given no matter what. Every person desires to be loved. Usually, parents love their children, but not all parents demonstrate it appropriately. Actions and words must match in our demonstration of love for our children. Spending plenty of time with our children demonstrates love and care and also gives them room to share in it. There are also other ways of demonstrating love. Appropriate touch starts with holding our babies and giving hugs as they get holder. Do activities together, such as reading together and helping them with homework. How you look at your children speaks volumes, because the eyes are the window to the soul. No matter how wrong our children are, we should refrain from looking at them with condemning or demeaning eyes. We should be intentional to communicate affection to our children by the way we look at them. Telling your children that you love them is very important. Using kind words when communicating and refraining from using damaging language is also important.

Why Unconditional Love?

"But God demonstrates his own love for us in this: While we were still sinners, Christ died for us. Since we have now been justified by his blood, how much more shall we be saved from God's wrath through him!" (Romans 5:8–9 NIV).

God gives us such an amazing example of unconditional love through Jesus. What we have in God is absolutely none of our doing or effort, but all is done for us by Him freely. His love for us is always complete and unconditional.

Many of the things we do in life are attached to a direct reward. For example, we go to work every morning because we get a paycheck to provide our daily needs like shelter, food, and clothes. On the contrary, the love and everything we do for our children must have no strings attached, which can make parenting feel like a thankless job. Think about the sleepless nights with a crying baby— the constant watch over your children, the worries, and the demands that follow as the children grow older. It is a lot to give, and many times it's a great sacrifice on the part of the parents. Yet, the only reward we should expect and trust for is that our children turn out all right. That is the description of unconditional love.

This can seem very simple, but by taking a closer look, we realize there are ways we can have unrealistic expectations from our children, which can lead to major complications. Parents who are broken and lonely can have a hard time giving unconditional love to their children, which is why the wholeness of parents' matter. For example, with unconditional love, parents are mindful to hold their child because the children need to be held. Lonely parents, on the other hand, may hold their children because the parents crave human touch. These parents will insist on holding their children even when they do not want to be held, creating unnecessary dependence on the children for the sake of the parents' emotional satisfaction. If we don't become intentional, it is easy to do things that cause our children to become overly dependent on us because it feels good to wait on them. As a result, we may forget to do things that foster their growth and independence to becoming who God made them to be.

Some parents become manipulative to keep their children from moving on with their lives because they lack the understanding of unconditional love. We are meant to raise our children the best we can and then release them to fulfill their purpose. Unconditional love always looks out for the best interest of the child and not what feels good to the parent. It feels good to love our children and care for them; however, that should not be the focus of the parent but the byproduct of doing what is best for the children. Focusing on the needs of the children and meeting those needs unconditionally makes it easier to include those aspects of parenting that otherwise seem difficult, such as discipline and boundaries. With unconditional love, everything a parent does for the children is focused on the well-being of the children, and the reward is the well-being of the children. This will bring about successful parenting and lasting relationships. The best way to keep our children close to us is not by manipulating them but by being great parents who help them become successful and productive.

Faith

"Fix these words of mine in your hearts and minds; tie them as symbols on your hands and bind them on your foreheads. Teach them to your children, talking about them when you sit at home and when you walk along the road, when you lie down and when you get up. Write them on the doorframes of your houses and on your gates, so that your days and the days of your children may be many in the land the LORD swore to give your ancestors, as many as the days that the heavens are above the earth" (Deuteronomy 11:18–21 NIV).

Raising a child in trust of God is crucial. We will not always be with them, especially the older they become, but God is always there with them and for them. The sooner you start, the better it is to maintain when they grow up. We find our purpose in our creator, and our goal is to fulfill our purpose. Instead of training our children to depend on us for their decisions as they get older, we need to train them to look up to God who is always with them wherever they go. They need to be solid in their faith to overcome tough times of life successfully and to remain sober during good and blessed times.

Studies also show that people who have faith handle life better. In sickness, people who have a faith respond better to treatment than those who claim no faith. Faith brings comfort, discipline, positive attitude, and many other attributes that help bring about the best in life. This is because it is the dependence on someone greater than ourselves. It is learning to depend on God who is real, who is mighty, and who has no limits.

Faith can come to any person at any time, but it is a great advantage to raise our children in faith, and it is the greatest legacy to give to your children. If your children have God, they have everything they will ever need or want in life.

Nurture Uniqueness

"For we dare not class ourselves or compare ourselves with those who commend themselves. But they, measuring themselves by themselves, and comparing themselves among themselves, are not wise" (2 Corinthians 10:12 NKJV).

No other child in the whole world is like your child. If you have two or more, you will notice even identical twins have their differences. I believe God made us each uniquely so that we can depend on each other. Every person has their strengths and weaknesses, and that is okay. However, something tends to happen as we grow up, and suddenly, we want to blend in. We do not want to stand out. We also find that we struggle with the few around us who are making efforts in a positive way to stand out. There is almost an unwritten rule that we expect to be the same. It might start with a child coming home and wanting something that everyone else in their class already has. Even though it is not necessary or the child has something different instead, we rush to get the item for our child to help them fit in. We are not made to fit in, and neither are our children. Yes, the child is hurting and crying because everyone has something your child lacks. The best thing is to talk to your child about it and discuss the importance of not copying others. Some things might be necessary to buy, but most of the time, the child can do with what he or she already has. Being firm, along with helping them understand how beautiful and strong they are to be themselves instead of copying helps develop acceptance of being unique.

It is important to keep in mind that each child's development is unique and complex. Oftentimes, we look around and compare our children with others their age. We then push them toward what we see other children doing ahead of our own. The expert has come up with general milestones that are predicted for each age group, but some children make their own rules as to when they hit certain developmental milestones. Environment greatly influences the development of children as well. For example, a child raised walking to school two miles every morning and afternoon develops great motor skills compared to one who takes a bus. A child raised with books and reading develops reading skills and a relationship with books differently than a child raised watching several hours of television each day instead of reading. Our goal as parents should be to develop the best of each of our children and not to make them be like someone else. Encouraging our children to accept being who they are helps them become solid, which helps them resist the temptation of bad influence as they grow older. Children who accept their differences at a young age can make great leaders.

Priority

"But seek first the kingdom of God and His righteousness, and all these things shall be added to you. Therefore, do not worry about tomorrow, for tomorrow will worry about its own things. Sufficient for the day *is* its own trouble" (Matthew 6:33–34 NKJV).

Life comes with very many things that will compete for you— your attention, your time, your resources, etc. Jesus clearly speaks to a need for setting our priorities right. Taking time as it comes will make you miss what is important to you. As a parent, your children should be your No. 1 responsibility. It is important to take some time and make clear to yourself what your priorities are and how best you will keep them at the top of your list because life won't keep them there for you. What life naturally does is keep us very busy so that we forget to pay attention to whether we are doing is important to us and our progress. For example, some people might spend several hours each day chatting over the phone with friends, while their children are put in front of the television to keep them quiet. Even though your intention is to be there for your children, your priority is your friends over your children in this case. Your children need you to talk with them much more than your friends do even though friends are important as well. Think about it. How many other scenarios also compete for your time over what is most important to us?

Communication

"'Come now, and let us reason together,' Says the LORD, 'Though your sins are like scarlet, they shall be as white as snow; Though they are red like crimson, they shall be as wool'" (Isaiah 1:18 NKJV).

God is so gracious, and although we don't deserve His mercy, He gives to us freely. God calls us to reason with Him, which means to communicate thoroughly until we feel heard and hear Him. It is the very same thing we need to aim at doing with our children.

Communication is one of the most important aspects of any relationship. Proper communication should begin at birth and be maintained throughout parenting. A child is a complex human being with his or her own mind. The difference is that the child is in a vulnerable state and dependent of the parents. Some parents flip the coin and depend of on the child to be in charge. To have a healthy relationship between a parent and a child, communication must be very clear, including, love, discipline, expectations, rules, who is in charge, boundaries, and all aspects of living together. It also includes day-to-day life like feeling, thoughts and ideas, school, friends etc. Communication is nonverbal, verbal, and two-way. It must all be understood correctly to foster strong, lasting relationships.

One of the most important aspects of communicating with our children is listening to them not only from their words but with our hearts. By doing so, as parents, we are communicating that the child is important and that we care deeply about who the child is. This involves giving children time to express themselves without showing impatience—for example, not finishing their sentences even if you know what they are about to say or showing respect for their immature thoughts. The more you listen to your children, the more they will continue to talk to you about their lives as they get older into the teenage years and then adulthood. When children feel shut down or like they don't matter to their parents, they find other ways to meet their needs. Once parents lose communication with their children at young age, it is difficult to recover it later in life. As difficult as it can be to listen to a four-year-old repeat the same story multiple times and call your name what feels like a million times a day, we must listen like it is the first time each time. Listen genuinely. They can tell when we don't, and it both hurts their feelings and destroys their trust. When children feel heard, their self-confidence increases. When they don't feel heard and valued, it reduces their self-esteem, which reduces their confidence in who they are. Children tend to internalize what is not working around them as their fault or believe it means something wrong with them, which destroys their core.

We must also talk to the children, each at his or her own level. Often, we must be ready to repeat what we already said, potentially multiple times, without showing frustration even with older children. We must aim at teaching them life lessons without making it obvious or lecturing them. Basically, as parents, we need a lot of wisdom, and the good news is that it is available for us when we ask for help from God, as well as study. Most importantly, be aware that how we live our lives communicates volumes to our children. Training means modeling and practicing what we teach.

One of the communication tactics that seems to work and reduce stress for both children and the parents is communicating ahead of events what the expectations are. For example, in case of an event, communicate to the children what the event is and as much as possible about it. Communicate what your expectations of the child are while at the event. The child goes to the event with his or her mind made. It helps the child find boundaries within your limits and without you causing commotion while in public. At the event, the parent might need to remind the child sometimes, depending on age, and it works out much better than trying to introduce rules and expectations at the event. The more the communication you maintain in your home, the better your relationships will be.

Commitment

"Now therefore, fear the LORD, serve Him in sincerity and in truth, and put away the gods which your fathers served on the other side of the River and in Egypt. Serve the LORD!" (Joshua 24:14 NKJV).

This scripture speaks to commitment with reverence to our God. It is powerful to think of our heart condition regarding our relationship with God. Which other gods are we holding to today? Is it our careers, possessions, things, people, or fame? In the same manner, which things have we exalted above our children? How seriously do we take our children and our roles as parents? Are our children one of the things on a laundry list of things to do when we get to them, or are they separate and a priority? How important is whatever is taking your time away from your children? What changes can we make to enhance our commitment to our young children while they need us the most?

To make the best out of parenting, you must be devoted to

the responsibility. Commitment isn't about feelings. There will be many times as a parent that you won't feel like doing what needs to be done for each situation. For example, disciplining your child is one of the things loving parents have a hard time doing. Discipline is painful, and although it may hurt your child's feelings now, it is necessary. Therefore, we must do it for the sake of our children even though we don't want to. Commitment is also about providing for your children until they are of age and able to provide for themselves. You can't wake up and miss going to work because you like a certain program on television and don't want to miss it. The moment you remember that missing work could cost you your job, the program doesn't matter anymore because it is more important to keep a roof over your children's heads. Commitment causes a parent to make big sacrifices without thinking twice about them. Our children are our responsibility, and we must be committed to them to create the best of their outcome.

Being Intentional

There is a certain way parents dream to see their children turn out. Being intentional means to *consciously* choose how you want to raise your children and then sticking with it throughout their growing years. For example, choosing values, habits, a positive outlook on life, and generosity, among others. Once a child is born, each parent imagines great things for that child's life no matter how good or bad the circumstances are at the time of birth. However, not all children end up in the places their parents dreamed about. How the children turn out isn't based on the circumstances they are born into as much as what is put into the children growing up.

Some children are born in great conditions and end up struggling with life, some even committing suicide as adults. Other children born under tough conditions end up thriving in their own lives. Being intentional increases the chances of your children thriving despite other conditions. You first start by purposely considering what your dreams are for your children. The next step is to deliberately decide how you as a parent can do your part in bringing that dream to reality and following through. That doesn't mean you get to decide what your children will do when they grow up. It is more dreaming of your children succeeding in whatever God will lead them to undertake, as well as maintaining their internal peace and security in who they are. Being intentional is hard work, because it is required every day in everything you do. But like everything else, practice of anything forms habits, which eventually become a lifestyle. Thus, it ceases to be work and becomes your normal way of life.

Discipline

"No discipline seems pleasant at the time, but painful. Later, however, it produces a harvest of righteousness and peace for those who have been trained by it" (Romans 12:4–11 NIV).

Discipline is a term that is used in various ways, but the outcome of it is always positive. We discipline ourselves to get the results we want in life. Discipline is also used to bring correction, especially in parenting. Whichever way it is applied, discipline is uncomfortable and can even be painful, but the results are always desirable. Most of the things we do in life that prosper us take living a disciplined life. For example, choosing to go back to college and pass examinations takes discipline. Writing a book, winning a basketball game, keeping our weight in check, and getting enough sleep regularly all take discipline. Therefore, discipline is a good word and a needed practice.

God in His love disciplines us and expects us to live disciplined lives. So must we discipline our children for their sake. Focusing on the outcome of discipline instead of how it feels makes it easier to do. Love and discipline go hand in hand. There is a great difference between discipline and punishment. Punishment is aimed at causing pain. Sometimes, punishment is not used for justified reasons. Some people use punishment for selfish and hateful reasons. Therefore, punishment should not be confused with discipline. It might work to bring correction in some cases, but it doesn't necessarily change the heart of a person against the wrong done. Discipline, on the other hand, is always aimed at correcting or being productive. When discipline is practiced and becomes a lifestyle, the suffering turns into joy for the results we achieve. To succeed in our goals, discipline is necessary. Children must be disciplined to be respectful, successful, productive human beings. For children, it involves correction and even consequences until they form the habits that are positive for them.

Discipline during Parenting

The greatest way to create discipline in your children is by spending a lot of time with them. Training takes care of most behavior issues. Children usually start by doing the wrong thing because they don't know any better. With proper communication and teaching, they understand and grow into appropriate behaviors. When correction is done right away, change comes easier than waiting to correct later. A child is never too young to be corrected. The moment the behavior shows up is a good sign that the child is ready for correction of that behavior. Some of the actions parents laugh at and think cute are the same actions that end up becoming big problems as the child gets old. The sooner correction happens, the better.

Depending on age, personalities, and situations, discipline should be applied as appropriate. Each child responds differently to correction, making it important to pay attention to what works best for each child. As much as possible, don't postpone disciplining, especially with younger kids. When you discipline immediately, the children are better able to attach the correction to the action. When you wait to correct, especially if you are in a party or a public place, the child forgets about the action by the time you get home. Trying to discipline later seems like punishment because the child doesn't attach the disciplining to the action and feels unfair to the child. No matter where you are, find a way to pull the child aside and correct him or her immediately. If that is not possible, let it go and look out for a more appropriate setting. Older children can be talked to later if the action happened in a place that did not give room for immediate correction.

Always aim at helping children understand how action will impact things later in life if not corrected. Help them change their choices and understand the consequences so that their choices are better down the road. The more children learn to be responsible for their actions, the better the choices they will make, which will lead to fewer behavior problems.

With work ethics, train your children to make a list of priorities. Teach them why they should choose to do their homework before playing or watching television, for example. Teach them to make healthy choices instead of doing what may feel good. For example, explain to them why it's unhealthy to stay awake on the phone or other gadgets instead of getting enough sleep, eat a lot of bread or other unhealthy foods, avoid vegetables, have party friends who lead them down the wrong path, and so forth. Help your children see the importance of choosing discipline for their lives instead of what feels good for the moment. Having discipline in life brings about desirable outcomes.

In creating discipline for your children, being defensive and protecting your children's wrongs doesn't benefit your children. Some parents get very defensive when informed of their children's wrongdoing by friends, relatives, of teachers. It is important to listen attentively to what others involved in your children's lives are saying and investigate to help them correct mistakes. For example, when others tell you that your child is taking other children's things, pay attention and help your child realize why that is wrong instead of getting upset at the people giving you the information. When bad behavior is not corrected and is instead defended, things become and eventually could hurt your child's life in ways that cannot be easily redeemed. Be open to receive information about your child, and view those sharing the tough information as your true friends instead of enemies, especially when you don't know for sure whether what they are saying is true. Aim at creating in your child the best behavior and discipline possible.

Decision-Making

Although we allow children to make age-appropriate decisions, parents are to remain the decision-makers for their homes. Parents make rules and give guidance to the children, and at no time should a child have equal say in the decisions of the home while they are growing up. When we train our children to respect our authority, they respect other authority in their lives when they grow up. If we train them to walk over our authority, they are unable to respect other authority, which often leads to trouble with bosses, teacher, and other authority figures. Maintaining your authority as a parent in your home from the time your children are babies through their growing years makes it easier as they get older, because that becomes their norm.

As our children get older, parents need to help them learn to make good decisions pertaining their lives. For example, how they choose their clothes when they get dressed and why, who to have for a friend and why, what activities to get involved in and why, etc. It is the parents' responsibility to train their children to make decisions for their lives that benefit them currently or in the future. Showing them by example and training them will make them responsible for their own decisions as adults. The greatest thing to instill is to think about why each decision is made.

Hard Work/Work Smart

Being a good parent takes a lot of work. As parents, we have ourselves to take care of, which is hard enough, and then other lives are dependent of you as well. That's tough. Once your babies is born, until you train them, they dictate when you wake up, when you sleep (if you do), when you shower, when you eat, and the like. You are constantly calculating your activities around their naps and feeding times. Then they start to crawl, and you are constantly watching their every move. Once walking starts, you are forced to put away all your tablecloths; otherwise, in a split second, everything on the table is pulled to the floor. Then you have a baby to worry about—has he been hurt? Plus, there is a whole mess to clean up regardless of the sleepless night you may have had. Every stage along the way has its challenges, and as a parent, you can't put any of it off for another day or year. It all requires attention as it happens, because every day has its own challenges.

To make life easier, we can make the choice to work smart alongside our hard work. Life is a school of learning, and if we are open, we can learn from various sources. Knowledge is power. For example, when my son was born, he stayed in the hospital for his first two weeks due to a medical condition. Within those two weeks, the nurses taught me that I could train my child to feed on a timed schedule, which is good for the child's feeding habits overall. It also creates structure for the parent, and planning becomes easier. I watched the nurses do it, and I saw that it worked. When I brought my son home after the two weeks, I continued what I had learned from the nurses. I did more studies on the effects, which I will share later in a different chapter. By the time he was three months old, he slept a straight six hours at night, and I did not wake him up to feed him. By six months of age, he slept a straight eight hours at night, which means I slept also, other than occasional quick checks while he slept. I fed him well during the day and let him sleep at night. This brought me great results in many ways that continue today.

I purposed to do the same with my daughter when she was born, and it worked. Instead of me feeding my children whenever they cried as babies and growing children, I purposed to feed them because they needed to be fed, and I planned it to make sure they were not too hungry at any time. That helped time wise in many other ways. I consider that as an example of adding working smart to hard work, and I truly believe it was best for my children's best interests then and later in life, as I will share later in the chapter on feeding habits. Accepting that parenting is hard work helps our attitudes toward parenting.

Boundaries

There is a difference between a parent and a child just like there is a difference between a boss and an employee, and boundaries must be clear to create health in all relationships. It is important to make it clear that you are the parent, and they are the children, which means you are in charge. Our children are not meant to be our friends, especially in their growing years. Authority in the home needs to be clear, which takes away confusion and constant wrestling between parents and children. That does not mean controlling children. It means setting clear rules, expectations, and respect to guide how the parents relate to their children. It also created an example for how they should relate to other authority figures outside of the home. Practicing healthy boundaries at home helps your children build healthy boundaries for their lives outside of home, including at school and work.

When boundaries are missing, respect is lost, and eventually, the relationship we are working so hard to maintain ends up lost. Children are easier to manipulate when they are young, which leads to some parents losing boundaries with their children. As children get older without boundaries, relationships become more challenging and what seemed like happy moments start to turn into constant conflict as a result of parents and children equal status in the home. Many of these parents then back off and let their children take charge with the hope of maintaining peace. This destroys the children in the end, and the relationship with the parents is lost because there is no respect between them. Many children raised without boundaries end up resenting and blaming their parents for their downfalls. While the parents' intention was to make their children, happy and have this fun relationship, it mostly ends up backfiring on both the children and the parents.

Practicing healthy boundaries at home trains your children respect, which makes their lives and relationships easier overall.

Consistency

How we raise our children should be done such that they know what to expect. Consistency means there are patterns that are predictable. For example, we discipline based on their actions and not based on our feeling. Discipline should not be given because a parent is angry. It should always be done to correct a child, which means it should be done even at the happiest of times when needed. The way we discipline should be predictable. The more consistent we are with behavior, the better the results we get. Consistent discipline produces character, which means there should be less need to discipline.

Consistency in prayer develops a lifestyle of prayer. It takes away confusion and fear, especially in young children. As Christians, we live our faith based on the word of God and not our feelings, which produces consistency in our walks. When children don't know what to expect, it causes instability and fear in them. Consistency causes children to be confident. For example, if there is not screaming and fighting in your home, your child comes home every day expecting a peaceful atmosphere, which gives them confidence. If there is screaming and fighting some days and happiness other days, the child never knows what to expect and is always disturbed even during those happy moments because experience has taught the child to be on alert for danger all the time. When parents are consistent in all their ways, they are easier to relate to and easier for their children to please.

Stability

Every child should have a place they call home, as well as stable relationships. Children need food, clothes, education, and relationships they can depend on. Unstable homes and marriages cause instability in the mind of a child. For example, when a father leaves abruptly for several days without a warning and comes back whenever he wants, it causes instability in the home and the child. In a stable home, a child knows he or she has a home and is not worried about being homeless or having a night without dinner. Basic needs are being met, and basic loving relationships are being maintained. The children know what to expect and are not disappointed regularly. The children know the people in their lives and this doesn't change suddenly and often. For single parents, it is important to keep your dating partners away from your children until there is a committed relationship. The more relationships you introduce to your children then change them, the worse it is for your child's emotional development. Each time your heart is broken by the loss of a partner, your children who trust very quickly are a lot more left broken. It is important to maintain stable relationships around your children. For example, involving family like grandparents, aunties and uncles and trusted friends etc.

Nurture Sibling Relations between Your Children

Our children need each other apart from us parents. Parents who are intentional about fostering healthy relationship between their children cause them to grow close to each other, which is helpful all their lives. Siblings love each other, but they also have conflict. They need to learn how to support their relationships and resolve conflict without us standing between them every inch of their growth. Whole parents don't have a need to be in between their children's relationships with one another. Parents who are secure help their children become secure in their decisions instead of controlling them and their relationships with each other. Sometimes, children get frustrated with their parents, especially those parents who are secure in their role as a parent and not a friend, and that is okay. Having a sibling to talk about their frustration is a safe place and healthy for them. When children have conflict between each other, give them space to resolve it between themselves as much as possible. Most of the time, they do if no one interferes with their process. In cases when a parent needs to intervene, be neutral and support their process. Say things that help them reflect—for example, "What could you have said differently?" or "I know you love each other so much that you want to work this out." This can help bring about a quicker resolution. In cases where one child needs correction, pull one aside and process with that child separately and then encourage that child to make things right before leaving them alone. Hovering over our children's relationships or taking sides does not foster positive development. It is important for parents to seek their own wholeness, because that reduces the chances of parents needing their children for their own emotional fulfillment. Wholeness in parents fosters wholeness in their children, as well as in others family relationships.

Being vs Doing

"Be still, and know that I *am* God" (Psalm 46:10 NKJV).

Very often, we lose ourselves in the things we do and are unable to enjoy being who we are. While it is good to encourage our children to succeed in school, activities, and other things they do, the most important thing we can instill in them is being content in just being. Our children need to be secure internally that we love them and accept them for who they are, not for being the best student in class or the best member on a sports team. Children shouldn't feel the need to earn approval of their parents by performance. They should perform because they are motivated from the inside based on who God made them to be and know they are accepted and loved for just for being themselves.

Unfortunately, learning to be content in being does not happen in business but in stillness. When we fill our children's schedules with activities and give them no time to reflect, they don't learn who they are at the core. When children wake up every morning and are on the run all day long, they learn to be performers and learn to be uncomfortable with stillness because they don't develop being in touch with who they really are. Our society has become uncomfortable with the stillness in which we find our true selves and contentment. We are trained to measure ourselves based on performance and have a nervous breakdown when unable to perform to our expectations.

It is important to train children to turn off all noises, stop all business, and listen. Pay attention on inside. Spend time every day by sitting and talking to your children about what is important to them. It might be a doll or feeling sad because a friend at school refused to talk to her. As a parent, get down to where they are and sit there with them. When schedules are fully packed with activities, we can't possibly have time for stillness with our children. Our children don't become strong at the core by playing all the sports available, even if sports are good for them. They become strong at the core by growing into being comfortable with just being as a starting point of everything else they do.

We can train our children to celebrate being by intentionally providing time for reflection, reading God's word (especially on identity in Him) and meditating on it, modeling personal prayer time, talking with them about unhealthy competition, and enjoying resting, among other things. When our children develop in this, they generally deal better with life, including failures and faith, because they know they are accepted for who they are and not because of a great performance.

Teach Them Gratitude

"I am not saying this because I am in need, for I have learned to be content whatever the circumstances. I know what it is to be in need, and I know what it is to have plenty. I have learned the secret of being content in any and every situation, whether well fed or hungry, whether living in plenty or in want. I can do all this through him who gives me strength" (Philippians 4:11–13 NIV).

Focusing on our blessings helps bring more blessings and helps prevent depression. We all have something to be thankful for and something we want. Focus on what is lacking can be draining and can cause vises like jealousy, unhealthy competition, and inability to celebrate others. A person who focuses on ways in which he is blessed stays peaceful, cheerful, and full of joy in spite of circumstances. We train our children by how we live our lives. When a parent is quick to point out blessings and rejoice in them no matter how small or big, children learn to do the same.

With that, comes the importance of speaking gratitude. The practice of saying thank you to God and others in your life opens more blessings. When people feel appreciated, they give more. God calls us to be thankful in all circumstances. Building trust in God helps develop gratitude because He works all things for our good. Sometimes things may seem to go the wrong direction in the natural, but God is working out something bigger. For example, when people we love walk out of our lives, we feel hurt and broken, but down the road, we may realize God was protecting us by moving them away. We might miss a ride or a flight and be upset just to find out later that it was for our protection. We need to do our part to the best of our knowledge and practice gratitude no matter how everything else seem to be going. It is for our children's good that we raise them with a spirit of gratitude in all circumstances. Contentment of the heart is not about having everything we want all the time. It is an attitude of the heart.

Self-Education

"My people are destroyed for lack of knowledge. Because you have rejected knowledge, I also will reject you from being priest for

Me; Because you have forgotten the law of your God, I also will forget your children" (Hosea 4:6 NKJV).

The more knowledge you have, the better your life gets. No matter what you undertake in life, learning about things helps you be able to handle life better. For example, when you or your child is sick, it is a good practice to understand the disease, medication, side effects of the medication, alternatives treatments, etc. The more you understand your situation or that of your child, the easier it gets to treat because you can explain things better to your doctor. You can also ask helpful questions if you study. The problem comes when you leave it to the doctors to figure out everything about us or our children. Likewise, in every area of our lives, we need to expose ourselves to as much knowledge as possible. In relationships, learn how men operate differently than women, how different personalities interact, and how raising boys differs from raising girls. This will help your marriage, which is good for your children, and you can raise children each for who they are meant to be.

Let Children Be Children

Children develop at different rates and act differently in each stage as they develop. Sometimes, parents command children to stop being childish, which does not make sense because children are meant to be childish. Children need to play and cry, and they need help and support. Children make messes, and that is part of learning and growing. Sometimes, it is tempting to do everything for our children to prevent messes and waste time, but this is not in the best interest of the children. The major part of parenting is training, which takes practical examples and turns them into a chance to do things for themselves and for others. Being overly critical of your children's way of doing things is not helpful either. Keep in mind they are children and encourage their attempts even when they are not perfect. Children don't learn things because they grow old but because they are taught to do things and given space to practice. The earlier a child is taught age-appropriate activities in life, the better.

Parents also need to let children be children by not overburdening them with cares of life. Maintain their innocence if possible. Protect them from negative exposure to things like violence and overwork. Exposing children to bad conditions is not what makes them tough. It instead destroys their emotional well-being, because they are not capable of dealing with major life difficulties. They develop negative coping mechanisms, which affects them as children and as they get older. Children need to be children until they grow up.

Children need a lot of patience to learn, ask the same question as many times as they need to, do their tasks, make mistakes, and do things their way, humanly speaking. For example, your twelve-year-old doesn't need to load the dishwasher the same way you do or put the cups in the cupboard the same spot you put them in. Be gentle with correction when needed instead of critical. Letting your children be children helps keep their keep their self-esteem healthy, which helps with their relationships and decisions in their life.

Be Patient

Due to the business of our lives, we can easily lay unrealistic expectations on our children. Children become easily distracted and are slower paced. They have nothing to worry about and run to. They live in the moment and enjoy everything that catches their eyes. No matter how busy we choose to be, it is not the children's problem, and we are making them pay for our choices when we don't consider how our choices affect them. To help our children learn healthy behaviors and responsibility takes patience. Sometimes, it's easy to deprive them of opportunities to learn because they are not moving as fast as we want them to. Parents choose to do everything just to get things done quickly at the expense of the child's learning and becoming responsible.

Children have minds of their own and will do everything differently. Some of what they do can be annoying, especially for tired parents. For example, children do a lot of things repeatedly and ask a lot of questions. They can spill multiple times a day, and when they try to dress themselves, they take their time. When a parent is constantly showing a child lack of patience, it affects a child's self-esteem and can result to shyness, shame, and feelings of inadequacy. Part of encouraging a child's confidence is being patient with them and allowing them time to do things at their own pace, listening to the same story they share over and over like you heard it for the first time, encouraging them when they spill or drop something, etc. Patience gives children the feeling that they matter to you more than anything else, which boosts their perception of their self-worth and increases their self-confidence.

Train Your Children to Read

Do you know people who say and believe their children don't like to read? The news is that most children left to themselves will not choose reading for fun. To get your children interested in reading takes more than buying them books, reminding them to read over and over, or even taking them to the library. Some of what parents do to get their children to read can seem like a punishment, which makes children resent reading all together. One secret to getting your children interested in reading is you as a parent reading with them and being enthusiastic about it. Talk about what you are reading together, and soon you will see your children looking forward to their reading time. While they are younger, reading books with them helps the most. If you continue the habit of reading with them into their teenage years, it might be that they read their book as you read yours and then you can listen to your children discuss what they are reading with you. It takes time and effort to train your children to read, but it is one of the most worthy practices you can develop in your children.

Reading has great benefits, including adding knowledge, but it is also a great exercise for our brains. The more we read, the sharper we keep our brains even into old age. Studies show reading regularly reduces chances of Alzheimer's disease; lessens reduces anxiety, stress, and depression and can increases relaxation and peace depending on what you read. Starting to read to your children before they are born or right after birth consistently helps them develop interest in reading as they grow up and can last them all their life.

The earlier your children learn to read, the better they are bound to do at school because it helps them understand problems better and faster. It especially boosts their self-esteem, gives them something positive to do in place of TV, video games and other screens that are not good for anyone especially children.

Advocating for Your Children

A parent should know their children better than anyone else. Whether it is at school, hospitals, or other places outside of home, parents need to be their children's advocates whenever needed. That does not mean excusing the children's bad behaviors when they need to be addressed. Being an advocate is different from being an enabler. Enabling is supporting our children's behavior when they are wrong just because they are our children. For example, when a child hits another child, some parents pick that child up and silently walk away like nothing happened or make statement like, "Children do such things," instead of correcting the child. Another scenario of enabling is when parents don't spend enough time with their children to know them well and defend them every time they are informed of misconduct. For example, when a parent is informed a child is taking other people's things or using bad language and responds by saying, "My child could never do that," and simply dismisses the situation instead of taking time to investigate.

Advocating means standing up for your children when things are going wrong—for example, when a child is being bullied and the school is not intervening, when a teacher has unrealistic expectations of your child, etc. Advocacy is difficult because we naturally like peace and would rather avoid confrontation, but sometimes it is necessary. Think about it. We are either hurting someone's feelings or letting our child get hurt, and many times we must make that choice.

Nutrition

What you eat makes a big difference in your health and largely determines your children's eating habits. Parents who eat vegetable automatically train their children to eat vegetables. What we eat makes a difference in how we feel and impacts our weight. Training your children to pay attention to nutrition and eating habits at an early age continues on into adulthood. Maintaining a healthy diet keeps your child healthy and is part of developing proper discipline. Guide them into choosing the right foods and the reasons for those choices. The more they understand and make it their choice, the longer they will stay with those choices even as adults. Along with healthy eating comes the importance of exercise and getting enough sleep. Our bodies need a healthy balance to last longer and be stronger.

Healthy Touch

A healthy touch brings about emotional healing and a sense of security for children. It is important for parents to hold their children whenever they need touch. Babies need to be held but also develop some independence when they are ready to be put down. Parents must be attentive to the needs of their children and provide these needs for their children's sake. As children get older and start to walk, they can go to their parents when they need to be held. They also let their parents know when they are ready to go. As a parent, the goal should always be providing for your children what they need and not trying to meet your emotional needs through your children. The more we give to our children freely, the more we train them to be givers. Healthy touch increases self-confidence, trust, emotional stability, and a sense of inner peace, along with providing affection for the child. Healthy touch from a parent also helps a child gain a sense of what unhealthy is touch as they get older. It's important for parents to talk to their children about what is not a good touch as they get older and become more independent. Children who have been given sufficient healthy touches and affection by their parents choose their relationships more wisely. They are better at staying away from wrong touches as they become older and more independent.

Children should not be ignored to teach them independence. Children should be given attention and comforted when needed. Children who can't speak communicate by crying, and the more attentive parents are when they cry, the more they trust their care and speak their needs when they are able. Healthy touch and affection are important to a child's development.

Be Intentional about Your Spiritual Home Environment

Have you entered a home or another place and right away felt uneasy? Other places may feel very peaceful and comfortable even if it is the first time you have visited. We are spiritual beings, although many times we don't think of it that way. The environments we are in either positively or negatively affect us and our children. Parents need to be aware and intentional about creating a peaceful, loving environment in their homes for their children.

If a home is full of sadness, children are bound to carry that sadness with them. The language we use at home and how we relate to each other affects the atmosphere in the home. If there is resentment, anger, or hatred, it can be sensed. Being intentional about the home environment keeps children peaceful and encourages better self-esteem and courageousness. One of the things parents need to keep in mind is that children don't have a choice when it comes to their environment. A husband or wife might leave the house for some time when the environment is not conducive, but children are always at the mercy of their parents. Other places the family goes also affects the children. Being intentional about the places you bring your children and the people you have around them helps keep them become peaceful and develop better habits.

Being Aware of the Subconscious Mind

The subconscious mind is always awake and active even when we are sleeping or not thinking much. The music we play and the things we see on television affect us even when we aren't paying attention to them. Sometimes, parents might think that children are too young to understand or grasp what is going on, but their subconscious minds soak in everything going on around them. This is a big reason we must be aware of the environment around us.

It helps to have a positive environment because the subconscious will then absorb the positive things going on. Having worship music playing as your children fall asleep, for instance, gives them a peaceful sleep, which helps them wake up in a better mood the following day. Listening to bad music or watching violence before bed causes disturbances to the mind and may cause children to wake up in a worse mood the next day. Sometimes, our children can develop fear due to the things they are exposed to without the parents thinking they are harmful. Some parents think children are too young to understand, but even when children don't understand, they are still affected. The younger the child is, the worse the effects are.

The things we are around the most slowly affect us. For example, staying around people who use bad language can slowly affect you, and unexpectedly, you might find that you use a curse word when under pressure that you never would otherwise use. Our subconscious is powerful and should not be ignored or undermined.

In Case of Adoption

"For those who are led by the Spirit of God are the children of God" (Romans 8:14 NIV).

When we become believers, we are adopted in the family of God. The process of adoption is that of becoming a child of God. Likewise, parents adopt children who become theirs. There are many adopted children who look completely different than their adoptive parents, including the color of their skin. How different the child looks is not what can cause problems for a child but instead how a child is made to feel in the home. Many adopted children develop problems with identity, depending on how they are raised. The feeling of belonging is very important for all children as they are growing up. How parents interact with a child who is adopted and how they talk about that child makes a difference in how accepted the child feels.

While God has adopted us into His family through faith, He does not constantly call us adopted children in the scriptures. Instead, He simply calls us sons and daughters. While it is important to education an adopted child on what it means to be adopted, it is not necessary to call the child adopted on a daily basis. It's not that it should be a secret, but the question becomes, why do we want everyone to know that our child is adopted? Why do we go into telling everyone we meet the child is adopted even when no one is asking? How does this daily introduction affect a little girl or a little boy who is trying to figure out who he or she is?

We might think we are being honest and forthcoming by always introducing a child as adopted, but that is not what the child is thinking. Tell the child about adoption and educate him or her on the subject so it doesn't come as a surprise when talking to others. Emphasize to you child that he or she belongs and then demonstrate that every day, including during introductions, especially when the child can hear you. If we only share the facts when asked, we might find out that we barely talk about the adoption. We can call our adopted children daughters and sons every day, which helps them much more than a daily reminder they are adopted. In many cases, parents introduce their children in a way that highlights the adoption—for example, "This is our firstborn, that is our second born, and that is our adopted child." And they do this right in front of the children. Instead, children should be introduced by saying something like, "These are my children," unless you are asked otherwise. Or, "This is our oldest son and our youngest son."

However, it is very important that parents tell the child the truth and give more information as the child asks when it is age-appropriate. It hurts children more to grow up without knowing they were adopted only to find out as adults. Telling children, the truth, supporting their growth, and helping them process through the mystery of their lives helps them accept themselves better. Repeating over and over to a child that he or she is adopted is not beneficial. Our Father does not call adopted children throughout the Bible. He calls us sons and daughters.

During Separation or Divorce of Parents

While children don't have a choice in the matter, they are the most affected and the least acknowledged in the case of separation or divorce. In most cases, there are two parents who are hurting and not in a good place emotionally to be able to support their children as needed. When parents are going through separation or divorce, children suffer in many ways. First, children hate it that their parents don't get along and part ways. Children often internalize things are being their fault and feel desperate to make things better for their parents with the hope of solving the problem and keeping them together. When that doesn't happen, which children have no control over, they are emotionally hurt, scared, and insecure. Many times, the children's need in this situation are left undealt with, and the children grow up with the burden of it, which affects them more than parents realize until it is too late. Children can develop behavioral problems in to communicate their hurt, gain attention, or be heard. Many times, these signs are ignored or children are punished to stop the behavior, which makes it worse or forces the children to shut down.

It is important to help children process their emotions during this time. Get them involved in therapy if necessary and spend plenty of time with them. Most of all, reassure them that it is not their fault their parents are divorcing or not getting along. Children need to know they are loved and that their parents will be there for them no matter what. Keep in mind that each child reacts differently, so give each child what he or she needs by having patience for each unique need. If the situation is very emotionally draining, get family members more involved with the children to provide them the emotional support you may not be in a place to provide. How you deal with your children in this situation will make a great difference in how much of an impact it will have on them. Many parents going through divorce or separation can benefit their children if they keep in mind it affects children and prepare ahead of time to cater to their children's needs going through it.

Communication is very important. Talk to your children as soon as you decide you are going to separate and take time to help them understand what that means—unless, of course, you are in a bad situation and need to keep your upcoming move secret. Your children are not going to like it no matter how much you explain it. Be patient with their process and carefully listen to them and watch for nonverbal communication. This should not be the time you try to win your children's love and support but a time to provide the children with what they need. Make respect a goal and keep anger and blame away from the children. Don't speak negatively about your spouse to your children, because children love both of their parents, and it hurts them to hear negative things said about a parent even by the other parent. Your child could end up resenting the parent who talks negatively about the other parent. Be as consistent as possible and avoid going back and forth with your decision to separate or divorce. Be decided by the time you bring your children in on it; otherwise, it becomes an emotional yo-yo for your children, as well as for you. The younger the children are, the more things can affect their emotional development. Separation and divorce is cruel to children, and they should be given attention and support to deal with the situation when it happens. Ignoring it doesn't take it away even when the children are not expressing themselves. They should be encouraged to express themselves in order to deal with things and heal appropriately.

Children in Abusive Homes

A child's emotional development happens in the earliest years of life. The first two years of human life are the most crucial for emotional development, and the following years continue to build on what was started as children get older. Children are very vulnerable and don't have the capability to handle stress adequately. When they are exposed to stressful situations, they start to develop negative coping mechanisms, which affect how they relate to others as they get older and can affect all their future relationships. Intentionally keeping our homes peaceful and joyful helps our children develop emotionally healthy, which benefits their lifelong way of relating to others. It also helps children understand what good situations are and how to avoid the tough situations.

Abuse in a home can be life-changing for children involved. The younger the child is being raised in abusive home and the longer it happens, the worse the effects of the abuse are on the child. Unfortunately, especially when children are very young and not able to express themselves, some parents believe the children are not affected or will get over it once they grow up. Many children raised in abusive homes end up in abusive relationships, because that is what seems normal even though it is not happy. Children raised in abusive homes often develop low self-esteem, experience shame, and have a negative self-image, which also affects their performance in life and their expectations of themselves. A child's standards for life usually develop based on childhood conditions. The better the standards they are exposed to, the higher the standards they hold themselves to. Most children who develop dependence on alcohol and drugs admit that the behavior was modeled in their homes growing up. What you do in your home will influence your children, and you can't wish it away.

Divorce and separation are best avoided as much as possible, but raising children in a home where parents fight all the time and abuse each other and the children is much worse than separating if things are handled appropriately. Children who see a parent being abused by the other internalizes that to be a normal behavior even though it is hurtful. Children can become bitter toward the abusive parent and become fearful and anxious from never knowing what to expect. Some children may become abusers themselves, and others become vulnerable to being victims of abuse in adulthood. For example, a boy who grows up watching his father abuse his mother can either internalize that to be normal behavior or can become bitter toward the father. A girl who watches her mother being abused regularly and not doing anything to remove herself from the situation can internalize that to be normal, which may lead her to be a victim. Many people hold onto abusive, even dangerous marriages due to a faith commitment and the promise of being together "until death do us part." The command for marriage is to become one flesh, and a person cannot abuse their own flesh.

As parents, we must keep in mind that we are examples for our children. We cannot live one way and expect our children to live better. Our actions affect our children's future choices for their lives. We must be intentional about the example we set for our children on what is normal and what is not normal and what should not be tolerated. Abuse is not normal and should not be tolerated.

"Therefore, a man shall leave his father and mother and be joined to his wife, and they shall become one flesh" (Genesis 2:24 NKJV).

MOUNTAINS AND VALLEYS

Life is a mystery that we cannot understand.
we are born in a world we have no control over.
when the sun shines, she shines as she wishes.
Right at noonday, the rain pours as it wishes.
I wonder time and time, and wonder never cease.
In midst of the wonders, wonderful God reigns

Mountains fall ahead, valleys beneath our feet.
we weaken and we faint as we climb up the mountains.
We stumble and we slide going down the valleys.
we choose no mountains and choose no valleys.
We hurt in the mountains and hurt down the valleys.
In the midst of our hurts, our God hurts for us.

Mountains and the valleys do not last forever.
A short while they may last leaving us stronger.
Pain is not forever, neither is sorrow.
while at our weakest, Jehovah is Almighty
We don't understand; our God understands
Our hope and our strength, rests in His might

Mountains are high, God is higher,
Valleys go deep, God goes deeper
Our tears get hot, Our Lord's tears were with blood.
In the midst of our hurts, Our Lord hurts more
We have no control; He has full control
Victory smiles at us as we hope in Him.

by Ann Makena.

PART 3

Single Parenting

This is when one parent primarily raises a child or children, and in most cases, it is the mother. It is harder to raise children alone than as a team. Single parenting is challenging because one parent is responsible for the children in all ways, including sickness and school, as well as providing, protecting, and everything else that comes with parenting. In many cases, single parents are dealing with conflict with the other parent, visitation, and behaviors with children due to conflicting household parenting styles and financial shortages among other things.

The children in a single-parent home may feel a lack of the other parent, ask difficult questions, and feel sad about their family situation. Although a single parent might have good family and friends to give support, at the end of the day, the single parent is alone with his or her children and dealing with issues of life. Many times, single parents are dealing with their own mental and emotional struggle—for example, death, divorce, abandonment, or the aftermath of abuse and domestic violence. Physically, they meet all the children's needs by themselves and are forced to work harder to make ends meet. There are many challenges that face single parents.

However, two parents raising children in abusive and unstable

66

circumstances, which is one of the causes of single parenting, is worse for the children and everyone else involved. It is possible for children raised by a single parent to thrive, depending on how intentional and committed the single parent is. When children are assured of love and given stability at home, a safe and peaceful environment, etc., they will likely, do well no matter who is raising them. To get the most out of single parenting, there are certain things a single parent can pay attention to in addition to the general parenting tips already discussed.

Acceptance

"To everything *there is* a season, A time for every purpose under heaven" (Ecclesiastes 3:1 NKJV).

Most single parents are not single parents by conscious choice. Therefore, it is usually devastating when it happens, no matter how it happens. Acceptance does not mean what happened was right or justified. Many dreams are lost, and many plans come to a halt. The longer we take to accept our circumstances, the longer we take to begin healing and start our lives over. Acceptance is the beginning of moving forward from that painful spot and start building your life with what you have. Although some dreams are lost forever, there are many other dreams that can be redeemed and brought to pass if we accept the situation. Lack of acceptance keeps us looking backward, while acceptance helps up move forward. To be a better parent, acceptance is the right attitude for you and for your children's sake.

Let God Cleanse Your Heart

"The Lord *is* near to those who have a broken heart, and saves such as have a contrite spirit" (Psalm 34:18 NKJV).

When a change takes place in our lives that was not planned, it has the potential to make us better or bitter, and it is a choice we make whether consciously or unconsciously. To live tied to the pain of what happened in the past derails us from moving into the future that God has in store for us. It might be an early death of a spouse, a divorce, or abandonment, but any cause of single parenting is painful and difficult to deal with. We need to find the strength to let go and be set free. God can give us that strength and help us if we open up to Him and ask Him.

Many times, we may need to make a choice to forgive situations that are unfair and people who don't deserve to be forgiven, but we do it for our own sake. Sometimes, we have many questions that we can't find answers for. Why does a young parent die, leaving their children motherless or fatherless? Why do people who claim to love us mistreat us or abandon us when we need them the most? Why do some people seem to have perfect lives, while others struggle? The fact is that life is not fair, and many bad things happen to good people. What is helpful is to let God heal our broken hearts and help us to have a purity of heart that gives us strength to move forward and become better and more peaceful parents. This will help us raise strong, positive children.

Take Individual Responsibility

"But now, thus says the Lord, who created you, O Jacob, And He who formed you, O Israel: 'Fear not, for I have redeemed you; I have called *you* by your name; You *are* Mine When you pass through the waters, I *will be* with you; And through the rivers, they shall not overflow you. When you walk through the fire, you shall not be burned, nor shall the flame scorch you. For I *am* the Lord your God, The Holy One of Israel, your Savior'" (Isaiah 43:1–3 NKJV).

As a single parent, you are more likely to go through many more challenges than a stable two-parent home. This is especially true for those single parents raising a child with medical challenges

Parenting Children into Wholeness

or disabilities. Trusting in God will lift you to higher heights than anything else in the world. You are not responsible for the missing parent—only yourself. In cases of divorce, abandonment, and other situations where the other parent is alive, it is possible to get stuck in competitions and comparisons of who is doing what or not doing what is expected. This is a waste of time and energy and does not do anyone any good overall. The fact is that no one can make another person do what they don't want to do let alone a person that is no longer in your life. Instead of being upset about what the other person is not doing right, pray for God's grace to focus on what you can do to make the difference. Pray for God's help in making the best decisions for your children as an individual and following through on your part. Let go of the past and focus on your future and the future of your children. Whatever you do for your children, allow God to do it all with you. Pray for your children that God will fill up the missing pieces while you do what you can. Accept support from family and friends who care about you and your children. Guard your heart from being taken advantage of, which, unfortunately, happens easily to people who are already broken at heart. Keeping a pure heart and attitude will give you energy to care for your children instead of wasting energy trying to get even with the other parent, hoping to make them take responsibility. Focusing on your personal responsibility and leaving everything else to God's care keeps you peaceful and joyful even in troubled times. How well you handle the circumstance will determine how well your children will handle it.

Help Children Understand They Are Not to Blame for the Circumstances

Children have a way of taking the blame for broken relationships and need help understanding it is not their fault things went wrong. All children want their parents together, and it breaks their hearts when things don't go as hoped for.

69

Many times, they try to take responsibility to make things work between their parents, which others often laugh off as cute. The fact is, our children need a lot of help and support adjusting when things go wrong between their parents or in cases of a death. Being intentional with giving them time and listening to them, as well as reassuring them, helps. When a relationship between parents is broken, often the adults are aware of their own hurt but unaware of their children's hurt and needs. Many children rise to protect their hurting parents, which makes many parents think their children are okay only to realize the destruction later. It is important for parents to show strength for their children so that the children can trust leaning on them.

Young children are not equipped to handle great negative emotions. They need to be protected through life occurrences to be stronger and more stable in their adult lives. Parents are responsible for their children mentally, emotionally, spiritually, and physically, even during times of their own crisis. Whenever we need help dealing with division in a family, we need to be aware that our children need more support than we do, although they may not communicate it. The good thing is children are resilient, and given proper attention, they can bounce back and strong from tough situations.

Help Build Their Self-Worth

Putting forth your best efforts for your children communicates volumes for their self-worth. Single parents who can communicate positively that they will fight for their children and sacrifice for them show how important their children are to them, which, in turn, builds a sense of worth in their children. Having conversations to empower them will go a long way to help. Listen to them and pay attention to the things they are hearing from other children so that you can redirect them. Tell your children that you love them and are proud to be their mother or father. They need to hear it and see matching actions. Show them they are your highest priority in life by being available to them when they need you. Train them how to deal with negativity from others at school and in their lives. More than anything thing else, train them faith in God and His word and spend a lot of time with your children. Your children need you more than they need their friends.

Keep Your Emotions in Check

Keeping the environment calm helps keep the children calm and peaceful. Times of major change can be very difficult both emotionally and mentally, whether it is due to divorce, separation, or death; dealing with the sickness of a child; or another tough situation. It helps to make a conscious choice about how we react to this kind of situation. When parents let their emotions run the show, it makes children fearful and anxious and can lead to emotional instability in children. Children can develop negative coping mechanisms, which can last the rest of their lives and cause them to struggle all their lives, because that is the immediate example they have as children. The fact is that circumstances may be very difficult, but a lack of self-control makes everything worse. We can be intentional about making the best out of the bad situations in our lives for our children's sake.

In day-to-day events, things happen that we don't like or even upset us. How we cope with these situations trains our children in how they should cope in their lives. Ignoring or suppressing our emotions is not healthy either. The best way to deal with our emotions is to acknowledge how we feel and purposefully make known what we need from others. It might be some quiet time or talking through it, or it might be some time to get away, pray, or exercise. Being intentional about dealing with our emotions is helpful for us, our children, and the situation we are dealing with.

Self-Care

A person can only give what she has. Taking care of yourself helps you take care of your children appropriately. To be a good parent, you can make the choice to clean up your inner person, which leaves you with more energy to care for others. Start by accepting where you are—e.g., anger and frustration with life—and then seek out counseling services, as well as mature believers to help support you with the healing process if necessary. Make yourself accountable to the people you trust by sharing how you feel and what you are dealing with day by day or as necessary. Staying aware of your feelings about and your struggles with, for example, separation and divorce, as well as seeking support, can help create calmness, which helps your children. It can also help hold life together.

Part of self-care is developing into wholeness and knowing you are complete. We don't need a spouse to become complete. We need to make a choice to strive for personal wholeness and self-appreciation as a single person. Taking care of yourself should be done for you and not to impress others, although it may. This also gives an example to your children of how they should treat themselves and how to claim time and space for their own personal care. Self-care leads to be better health and more productivity in life.

Realize You Can't Make Up for the Missing Parent

Sometimes single parents struggle with guilt due to the absence of the other parent. Thus, they make it their mission to make it up to the children. Unfortunately, being led by guilt causes parents to make wrong choices, such as letting the children control the home, giving into everything the children demand, and the like, which ends up destroying the children's morals. It also has a potential to destroy other life relationships when they are grown, because the children develop entitlement. We can't make up for the other person.

We can only do the best on our part and trust God to make up what is missing.

Keep in mind what you what kind of people you would like your children to grow up to be. This helps in making simple, day-to-day decisions about how you deal with your children. It can help stay purposeful with parenting and keeps one from flowing with emotions. For example, disciplining children, especially when they are in a hurtful situation, is never fun. Yet, if we don't discipline them, the cruel world will do it the hard way. We love our children. As much as possible, we would like them to be loved and accepted by others. It's important to realize this will not just happen because you want it to happen. Therefore, love them enough to raise them for the world. Train them to respect authority, and this starts with us—the parents.

Start every aspect of parenting as soon as a child is born to solidify the positive example sooner. As a Christian believer, build them up and teach them what the Word of God says about their existence. Let them to know they are at the top of your priorities without doing it out of guilt. Let them know they are special to you and that other people's children are very special to their parents too, because that promotes respect for others. Keep in mind some of the cute behavior we laugh at now can be a problem tomorrow, so it's important to deal with those things early on. Don't let your children believe they can have their way in everything, because that is not true in real life. Raising them to become productive in the future can help them function better in this tough world. We can't make up for what is missing, but we can make the best of what we have.

Set Standards for Your Life and Your Children

How we treat ourselves is most likely how we train others to treat us. How we treat our children is most likely how we train others to treat them. Being a single parent does not make a person desperate.

Our choices do, whether consciously or unconsciously. This leads us back to finding wholeness, which is important because if we don't set standards, we tend to fall on anything that comes our way. As single parents, we must set standards by choosing who we allow into our lives and our children's lives.

How others see you treat your children is how they will most likely treat them. For example, if you are a mother who yells at your children and then remarries, your new husband will most likely not treat your children better than you do. On the contrary, if others watch you treat your children with kindness and dignity, they will most likely do the same, and if they don't, it's important to look back at your choices regarding who you allow into your life. Setting standards will also inspire your children to set their own standard as they grow into adulthood. Parents are the first and closest role models for their children.

Develop Your Faith

The best way to train children in the faith is by living it. Taking time to read the Bible, pray, and fellowship with other believers helps in faith formation and development. God is real and powerful, and the more we get to know Him, the better it is for us and our children. It helps us deal with life's situations better when we can slow down to pray and get God's guidance instead of getting things done in our human strength. It keeps us calm and peaceful to know there is someone greater who we can lean on and trust with our lives. It gives us a purpose and satisfaction in our lives. It gives our hearts the fear of God and keeps us away from making bad choices. Training our children in faith helps them get through anything in their lives.

When no one else can be close enough, God is always there. Developing faith in God helps keep sanity in troubled times. Pray for children instead of worrying about them. Pray concerning your needs whether it is for finances, stability, peace, or the right people in your life. God has ways to meet our needs that we can't fathom. Taking our children to church helps them learn some useful life principles, but living out our faith is what makes the greatest impact on our children's faith life.

When Finances Are Tight

Single parents usually have a harder time making ends meet. One thing to keep in mind is that our children need our presence with them more than they need our money and things. There are ways of living a fulfilled life with little money. For example, children will enjoy playing with an empty shoebox as much as any other toy. What matter the most is the parent is involved and enjoying what they are doing. Healthy food can be affordable if we keep our focus on nutrition and health. Simple outings to the park and play places that don't cost money are fun enough for children. Children don't look for price tags, they seek after love and acceptance. Your children value the time you spend with them more than the things you buy for them.

Get Educated on the Missing Pieces

As a single parent, it's important to understand as much as possible the needs of our children. For example, a single mother raising a son needs to be aware that her son cannot be raised like a girl or with expectations of a female. Reading books about raising a boy will shed a lot of light on how boys think and what boys need. One of the things you need to realize as a single mother is you could be a great mother to your son, but you couldn't provide the male-specific things that every child needs (although not every child gets). The same is true for single fathers. This can be devastating at first, and prayer helps bring peace through God-given ideas. For example, we can involve close family of the opposite sex to help nurture in our children what we can't naturally provide. Without reading and making ourselves aware, it is easy to raise our children with unrealistic expectations as single parents. It is not in the child's best interest to raise a boy with the expectations of a girl or vice versa. One caution is to not get children involved in parents' dating relationships in an attempt to fulfill the missing pieces. Children trust easily, and each time a parent brings a new person to meet them, it is an opportunity to leave the child more broken when the person leave. It is important to keep dating relationships away from our children until the case of a committed relationship.

More Sacrifices and Harder Work

While it is hard work to raise children even with two parents, it is more work to raise them as a single parent. The earlier a single parent accepts the harder work, the better it is for them and the children. It takes away the complaining and negative attitude toward being a single mother, which can lead to resentment toward the children. Some parents blame their children for being born at the wrong time. This is not fair to the children, because they have no choice in the decision to be born. Single parenting is difficult, but with intention, children can thrive. Like all other parenting, teaching children age-appropriate responsibilities will help them grow up right. Be intentional about not making your children suffer guilt for having to work hard for them. It is every parent's responsibility to work hard for their children.

In some ways, single parenting can be easier when a parent is stable instead of there being two emotionally struggling parents. A single parent can make rules and have fewer contradictions in maintaining the rules in the home than some two-parent homes with parents who lack unity. Single parenting is difficult but can have some advantages over some two-parent homes, depending on the attitudes of the parents involved.

Shun Away Shame

Single parenting can have shame attached to it, especially in cases of failed marriage or unplanned pregnancy outside of marriage. No matter how a child is conceived or born, the child is innocent and deserves the best that life. Holding onto shame as a parent keeps us from being the best parents we can be. While feelings will sometimes come without effort, it takes a conscious decision to fight against some of the emotions that hold us down. God forgives us, and we ought to forgive ourselves and let go of things we can't change. Women especially can be victims of shame, paralyzing them from becoming who God made them to be. It also affects the children and causes them to be ashamed of themselves, even if it is not the intent of the parent. Children can sense emotions, and shame can be a stronghold if not dealt with appropriately. All children need to be celebrated, and they somehow know when they are not, which affects their self-esteem and leads to difficulties in making their decisions in their future. Parents should verbally tell their children they are proud of them and show it in action. Parent who are ashamed of their circumstances are not free to bring their children in public and celebrate them in public. Some societies can also hold single parents down, especially single mothers, and it takes a you as a person to fight it the stigma. You are not less because you are a single parent. Your children are not less either. You matter and your children matter like any other child.

Strong Boundaries

There need to be a clear understanding between the parent and children on roles. A parent must remain a parent, and the children must be allowed to be children. It is very common for single parents to innocently let a child, especially of the opposite gender, to slip into the role of the missing parent. Parents unaware of the responsibilities their children are taking on may think it is wonderful or cute, but children are not developed enough to take on the role of a parent. Some parents may innocently start to benefit from their children emotionally, and this changes the parent-child relationship and turns it into an unhealthy situation, especially for the child. Single parents must be very self-aware and seek equal relationships with other adults in order to keep healthy boundaries with their children. Children feel safer and more protected when they can depend on an adult to love them unconditionally. They also learn to function better when there is clear guidance and rules. Parents should set the home rules, and children should follow those rules. Maintaining healthy boundaries when your children are young helps maintain them when they are in teenage stage.

Love comes with discipline, and we shouldn't be afraid to hurt our children's feelings at the expense of their lives and futures. It helps to encourage them to verbalize their feelings and kept that going. Another important aspect to keep in mind is that the relationship you develop with your children remains for a lifetime. Developing unhealthy relationships puts relationships in jeopardy as the children get older. Children have their own minds, and they get stronger in who they are as they grow. When we don't set boundaries early, things often turn sour as children grow and demand change. Children relate to parents the way they are trained. A child who has assumed the role of a mother or father in the home feels misplaced when the parent decides to remarry, which can be damaging to all relationships involved. When we stay strong for our children and keep the boundaries clear, relationships develop well and remain strong into adulthood.

Teach Children Respect for the Other Parent

"Honor your father and your mother, that your days may be long upon the land which the LORD your God is giving you" (Exodus 20:12 NKJV).

There is a difference between safety, respect, love, forgiveness, boundaries, and other things we need to develop for our sake. It does not matter what the situation is between the parents, God's commands are established. When we train our children to disrespect the other parent, we are causing them to miss God's blessings no matter how many excuses we find for it. This is one of the reasons we need our inner healing and awareness as parents. There are situations where safety is a concern. We must find ways to ensure safety and still train our children to respect the other parent. Teach them what the word of God says and why they must keep their attitudes pure in spite of the circumstances.

Avoid talking disrespectfully about the other parent around the children. If there is anything the children need to know for their own safety or understanding, share it respectfully at an age-appropriate time. Do not call the other parent names or make demeaning statements around your children. This hurts the children more than it hurts the other parent. If the other spouse is remarried, train your children safety, boundaries, and respect for them as a couple. This may not feel like it is possible in some situations, but meditating on God's word and understanding the benefit this brings to your children makes it doable.

Encouragement to single parents: Do your part diligently, and watch God do His part. I believe that many times God wants to bless our lives, but we are not ready when our blessings show up, so those blessings leave. I have met people who had relationships that started out beautifully but ultimately did not work out because the children were not trained to know what their position was. Children should always be children, and parents should always be parents, whether in two-parent families or single-parent families. The moment those roles are misunderstood, the future of many relationships is in jeopardy. The party responsible for defining these roles is the parent, not the child.

I believe you can do anything you put your mind to. We have more potential than we put into use.

I AM A CHILD LIKE THOSE OTHERS

I am different, I look different, I sound different.
I walk different, I eat different, my chair is different.
My uniqueness is unique, making me different.
But deep inside, I am a child like those others.

Don't be afraid of me, for I am harmless.
Don't stare at my differences; look into my eyes.
Don't change your voice like you speak to babes.
My need is acceptance in spite of my difference.
For deep inside, I am a child like those others.

Be yourself around me, for I know when you aren't
Be not strain, trying to think how to approach me.
Be only what you want, others to be to you.
My longing is genuineness, for that I can depend on.
For deep inside, I am a child like those others.

Deep inside, I long for relationships like others
Deep inside, I long for company and not pity
Deep inside, I long to feel valued, not like a burden.
My deepest longing is to be loved for who I am
For deep inside, I am a child like those others.

Smile at me whenever you can, that lifts my spirit
Give me a hug whenever you can, I rarely get a touch
Play with me, laugh with me, talk to me, listen to me
See beyond my differences; you will then see me
For deep inside, I am simply a child like those others.

By Ann Makena

PART 4

Advanced Parenting

The term *advanced* means at a higher level than others. All children need a lot of care, but some need more for various reasons. In that case, advanced parenting is raising a child who requires more care than most children. This parenting involves a child or children that may have chronic illness or a tough medical condition, a disability, etc. There are many things to keep in mind to get the best results for all our children when involved with advanced parenting. This includes the child needing more care and your other children in the household who also need regular care. All children in the household are special in their own way, and each, individually, must be given consideration for the sake of them all.

What tends to happen many times is the squeaky wheel gets the grease. In this case, the child needing advanced care receives most of the attention. The other children are either expected to understand or, worse, reprimanded for seeking attention because their situations are not as bad. In other cases, the child with advanced needs is resented by the parents and overlooked, especially in situations where the need is greater. This does not come about because the parents are bad people or because they don't care. It mostly comes about unconsciously, when parents aren't aware of what is happening within their own parenting. Many who deal with any form of advanced parenting are worn out from the care required of them. Unless they think ahead or come to their senses, it is easy to miss some important needs of their children; either the one with advanced needs or the other children in the household. This can be avoided.

Every child is important and must be made to feel they matter, especially to their parents and other adults in their lives. This can be done once parents are more intentional about it. It seems like a lot more work thinking about it, but it produces better results, which makes it more joyful. The other thing to keep in mind is that parenting lasts for a short period of time compared to the rest of our children's lives when they will use what we poured into them. Other things that come with being intentional are better behaviors and more acceptance, and generally, when people feel valued, they perform better. The same is true of our children. There are some tips that may help make the situation better for advanced parenting.

Acceptance of the Situation

"Trust in the LORD with all your heart, and lean not on your own understanding; In all your ways acknowledge Him, And He shall direct your paths" (Proverbs 3:5–6 NKJV).

This does not mean settling in and being hopeless. It is coming to terms with the fact that you are dealing with a situation that is more complicated than usual. You aren't in denial of the situation or minimizing it or its effect on you and the rest of the family. It is acceptance that more will be required of you and deciding to be intentional on giving your best while you care for yourself to remain on your feet. When you accept a situation for what it is, it becomes a starting point to finding the right solutions. It becomes easier to come up with a plan on how to go about it the best way possible. This includes our spiritual growth through the journey. It doesn't mean we stop expecting a miracle or God's intervention. It means remaining positive and praying for what we desire to see happen while we do our best with what we have. It means studying scriptures to see what God says about our situation and taking steps of faith as led by Holy Spirit while remaining peaceful with what we see in the natural. It is trusting that God has our best interest at heart even when it does not look like it.

Once a parent accepts the situation, it becomes easier for the children to accept it with the help of their parents. It makes it possible to live positively with the situation, which makes it easier for other people in our lives to come along and support us. When we are in denial or explaining away our situation, it a sign that we are uncomfortable with our situation, which makes others uncomfortable. Most importantly, once you accept, you can help the child with the difficult situation live positively, which makes a difference in the child's approach to life.

Giving Up Control

"'For My thoughts *are* not your thoughts, nor *are* your ways My ways,' says the Lord. 'For *as* the heavens are higher than the earth, so are My ways higher than your ways, And My thoughts than your thoughts'" (Isaiah 55:8–9 NKJV).

It is possible to accept a situation but lack peace about it. One of our worst pitfalls is having a need to fix the situation or carry the burden of trying to understand why. There is a difference between being diligent and being fixated. Many times, things happen that we have no control over. There are many things we shall never understand. Learning to surrender to God and letting Him be in charge while we do our best is a great way to handle a tough situation. It takes a lot of energy to keep our minds busy trying to understand why things went wrong while there is nothing we can do even if we understood. It is okay not to understand everything, and it is for our sake that we forgive what needs to be forgiven, especially when it isn't fair. Getting fixated on the situation and figuring it out takes away from being healthy as a person, as well as from proper parenting. Even better, it helps to see yourself as assigned by God to take care of His children. Once we remove ourselves from being in control and feeling life is unfair, we are healthier and can give better care. After all our lives are not our own, and neither are our children's lives ours.

Self-Care

"Do you not know that your bodies are temples of the Holy Spirit, who is in you, whom you have received from God? You are not your own; you were bought at a price. Therefore, honor God with your bodies" (1 Corinthians 6:19–20 NIV).

As a caregiver, it is important to allow time for self-care spiritually, emotionally, and physically. No vehicle runs without gas, and neither can we, although we sometimes deceive ourselves that we can. Many times, this is something we must be intentional about because the situation can lead us to see no way of doing it. Caregiver parents can carry a lot of guilt about what they didn't do right in certain situations. Getting away for self-care can feel like abandoning a child who needs you. To give our best to those who need us, we must give ourselves permission to refuel by taking care of ourselves. Our loved ones will understand, and if they seem not to understand, lovingly talk to them about it. It helps to take time for prayer and read scripture and other inspirational materials, exercise, reflection, and even rest. It is very important to get enough sleep and eat right to keep up. The more intentional we can be about our self-care, the better parents and advocates we can be for our children, especially when dealing with advanced parenting.

When we don't take care of ourselves, it is easy to be overwhelmed with care, lose patience, and be crabby, which can lead to depression. When a person is in that state, they cannot be a good parent or caregiver, although that is the heart's intention. Giving up control helps parents trust others to help so that they can take care of themselves. We take care of ourselves so that we are better and so that we have more to give to our loved ones.

Your marriage

In many situations where there is family member with advanced needs, especially a child, marriages are easily affected. The stress of raising a child with advanced needs is real and should not be underestimated. There are also marriages that grow stronger and thrive through these situations. How we deal with stress determines greatly the results of our relationships. We need to keep in check the expectations we have of our spouse and others. We also need to allow each other to be and not control the situation without consideration of our spouse. Both parents are affected each at their own level and each deal with the situation differently. Accommodation of our differences strength our bonds. Give each other opportunity to use operate within our strengths. Work together as a team each using their strengths and covering for each other's weaknesses instead of accusing each other. The better you work on your relationship the easier it gets to care for your child as well as build your marriage and family.

All Our Children

All our children are special and have a purpose for being and, therefore, should all be taken seriously. Thinking of each child as an individual and making a commitment to understand each with his or her own gifts and needs will help in raising each one, yet all of them together. Our children need each other as siblings, and how we raise them greatly determines how their relationships will be. As we raise each child to fulfill his or her God-given purpose, it is important to also promote relationships with each other, which is beneficial throughout their lives. With advanced parenting, this can be challenging, although it is possible with intentionality.

Think of real life. What happens around our places of work, churches, social gatherings, etc.? Our goal as parents should be to raise all our children, as much as possible, in such a way that they can function effectively in real life. Therefore, it is important to help each child learn to accept his or her condition and live with it positively without affecting the rest of your household. Some parents change everyone's lifestyle in the home to match the child who needs advanced care to avoid hurting anyone's feelings. This doesn't help that child or the siblings in the long run. For example, if one child is on a strict diet, everyone else in the house must eat what that child eats. There are many problems that come up with this practice. This can lead the child with advanced needs to feel entitled and expect everyone else in life to stop for them. This does not help the child develop healthy habits to function effectively in real life. Another negative effect is that the siblings and parents can become resentful of the child, leading to relationship complications. It is most helpful to the child with advanced needs to develop inner strength for coping with their differences rather than external temporary comfort.

In this section, we will address raising children with advanced needs, as well as the other children in the household. For use along with other tips from general parenting, this section will be more specific to advanced parenting.

Raising Our Child with Advanced Needs

Beyond the label is a buried diamond.

Labels paralyze the human minds even without physical impairment. Imagine how much more it does to children with advanced needs. As parents, if we can look past the condition and see the person in our child, it is possible to turn hopeless into hope.

There are many people walking on the streets and being productive while they are seriously sick until they find out they are sick. Our psyche is extremely powerful, and how we think about ourselves affects our lives more than our physical ability or disability.

Your child may be given a label—for example, disabled, autistic, or ADHD—based on medical evaluation or testing. As a parent raising your child daily, it is your responsibility to evaluate the potential of your child and do what you can to bring the best out in his or her life. Unfortunately, many people in life settle for the label and look for every little sign that reinforces that label. Many parents confess that label daily upon the child even when the child does not look like the label or act like the label given medically. Focusing on who the child is instead of a medical condition produces the best out of the child. Many children with advanced needs are not given the opportunity to use and develop their potential. Instead they forced by those in charge, such as parents and teachers, to match up to the label because that makes life easier for others. Many children are left unfulfilled and live sad lives due to the feeling of being a burden instead of being celebrated for who they are.

As a parent, you have the power to make a complete difference in your child's life and how that child handles his or her need in spite of the label. It doesn't mean denying a condition that exists. It means accepting it and denying it the power to control your child's life. It means making the best of your child's life and helping that child maximize his or her potential, which could result in greater productivity than most others. Our circumstances don't determine our destiny unless we allow them to. Our attitudes determine how high we go in life.

Spiritual Development

The spiritual development of your children is the greatest thing you can instill in them. Living out your faith daily helps your children develop theirs better and more profoundly. Faith helps your children deal with life circumstance better than going it alone. When a child has advanced needs, faith helps that child know there is someone closer than a sibling who is always nearby. It helps the child seek his or her purpose and find fulfillment in life even with the suffering or the shortcomings. Jesus did not fit in and had many sufferings in life, but He was always fulfilled in doing His Father's will. Our children can find the same fulfillment by learning to trust in God. You can help your child develop spiritually by reading the Bible together regularly, going to church together, praying together, and talking about ways God is working in your lives.

Nurturing Emotional Development

Having a medical condition that sets you apart is never easy, especially for a child. Children want to be children and to be around other children. Children want to be free to play, to love, and to be loved. Children want to feel accepted, especially by those who are part of their daily lives. It is hard to limit a child from being a child, yet sometimes it is necessary. You can be intentional about providing friends who are good for your child when a child is limited in activities.

It also makes a big difference to teach your child personal responsibility. This can be done by talking to your child about his or her condition and how to be protective. Help your child's confidence by helping him or her understand the condition and encourage your child to be confident in who he or she is. How your child perceives the condition will make a greater difference in life than the condition itself. Spend as much time as possible with your child, listen to your child, and show your child he or she matters. Normalize the condition and suffering as part of life. Encourage your child to be expressive and expose your child to other people with difficult situations, especially those handling it positively. Help your child understand that it is normal to feel sad and discouraged sometimes, and the important thing is learning to go past those moments and see the daily victories of life. Practicing positive confessions for your child will help him or her keep a positive outlook on life.

Family and friends are an important part of our children's lives. The more positive relationships a person has, the better it is for his or her emotional stability. Be intentional about involving family and friends in your children's love. Help your children become givers to others. This gives them a sense of purpose, which help them feel better about themselves. For example, sign them up for volunteer programs where they can help other people who need help.

Helping your children be as independent as possible also helps them feel better about themselves. They feel prouder of themselves when they can do things for themselves than depending on you as a parent to do everything for them. Whatever your children can do for themselves, train them to do those tasks and let them do those things. If they have younger siblings, train them to be of help to them. The more responsible children with advanced needs can be, the better they feel about themselves. The greatest thing is to be available to them and show them they matter to you by listening to them and comforting them. The healthier children are emotionally, the more energy they have for dealing with life, and then they can be productive, leading to a better self-image. The cycle then continues.

Raising a Victor in Your child

Victory is found in having ability to turn around what is difficult into a blessing for yourself and for others. A child with advanced need can be viewed as less likely to be productive and a blessing to other. However, it's often those children who have the greatest potential to become great blessings with the right push and support. Many people are suffering and in pain, and it takes a person who has suffered pain to give the support needed most of the time. It is the very reason Jesus is easy to embrace. He suffered pain and can relate to our pain. Likewise, people who have suffered pain can easily relate to others in pain and have a sensitivity that no school or theory can teach. When your child realizes he or she can turn around a personal difficult reality to help others, it creates the spirit of a victor within and gives that child a reason to battle for life. It might be something as simple as making friends with an elderly person in a nursing home and becoming a regular visitor that makes a difference. That gives your child a purpose to make him or her smile, knowing he or she is a blessing to someone else. Victory for each child varies just as uniqueness is for each person and children should never be compared.

I would like to share a quote from my book *Knowing and Yielding to the Voice That Counts* in this regard. I raised my son Nate partly as a single mother before I got remarried, and I believe whether you are a single mother or married, being intentional is what makes the greatest difference for your children. When I shared what I did to encourage the spirit of a victor in my son, I had no idea what he was going to do with his life, but I could see it was making a positive impact on how he felt about himself. Nate became an author at the age of fourteen and is encouraging many with his testimony. Because, as a mother, I believed in him and helped him believe in himself, he looked past his suffering and found a way to inspire others instead of having self-pity. I believe any parent with great intention can turn almost any situation around for their children with prayer, God's guidance, and hard work. Below is my testimony. You can apply the same principle differently depending on your situation if you find it helpful.

As Nathanael continued to grow, he became self-conscious when other children asked him about the scars on his head. He asked if he could start wearing a hat to cover his head. I did not think it was a good idea. What about the people without a leg or an arm? What about the person whose eye has been removed? I did not want my son to feel ashamed of the scars. Prayerfully, we started working on this matter together. I found articles to share with Nate about people who had physical things they could not hide and how they overcame their limitations and embarrassment. Nate and I talked about Jesus and how He was beat up publicly. We talked about the scars on His body. I encouraged Nate to think of how powerful it could be if he inspired people through his own story. If he covered the scars on his head, no one would ask about them. Leaving them uncovered gave him an opportunity to tell others what God has done for him. I encouraged him to express his feelings, which we then processed together.

Nathanael does wear hats, but not for the reason he originally wanted to wear them. He likes hats and will wear them on occasion, but he has become very comfortable with his scars. He stops to respond positively when people ask about his scars, which happens often. He is growing into wanting to share his testimony to give God glory for how far He has brought him. More and more, Steve and I see evidence that Nate is proud of himself, especially when he gets an opportunity to testify about God and how he deals with his struggles.

At home, Steve and I continue to teach Nate age-appropriate life skills. He continues to be positive and does not grumble when he is asked to put away dishes, to load the dishwasher, or to do any other chore. As great big brother, he helps his sister out as well. She adores him. My husband has taught Nate how to ride a bike and how to swim.

They also do male-specific things together. Steve is very deliberate about keeping Nathanael safe while they are hanging out together, which Nathanael loves to do. Steve is a great role model for what a man is supposed to be for his wife and for what a dad should be for his children. Nathanael has made comments like, "I wanna learn to cook so that I can help my wife out when I get married."

Living amid a community of people is important. Steve and I talk to Nate about the law and the importance of respecting the law of the land. We keep strong boundaries at home and train Sally and Nate to exercise simple respect at home. I believe that children should respect their parents, because that is the base for human life. I believe that if a child can learn to respect his parents when he is young, he will most probably respect those in authority when he is grown. I do not want my children to grow up with the mentality that they can do whatever they want to do in life. Life is full of rules and boundaries. I want my children to learn to keep to their own space while they are young so that they don't get lost when they step out into the rough world. Although Nate has endured about 20 times of brain surgeries as well as battle with seizures, he is productive and does not have self-pity. I must admit this has taken intention on the part of parents by God's grace. We all can bring the best out of our children by becoming more intentional about how we parent.

Your Other Children/The Siblings of the Child with Advanced Needs

While advanced parenting involves raising a child who has more needs than others, the other children in the home require great care, and overlooking this causes problems. We must be conscious that every one of our children is special and pay attention to making the best of each of them—all of them.

The siblings deserve to have their lives and should not be put through unnecessary suffering because the other child is suffering. As a parent, being conscious that your other children are already suffering from watching their sibling suffer and helping them cope with that is important. Help them process what they are feeling and what other children, maybe at school or at church, are saying about their sibling that might be disturbing to them. Normalize suffering to them and help them find positive ways to support their brother or sister without having to give up their childhood or life enjoyment totally. For example, have other family or friends watch over the child with advanced needs while you take the other children to the park or for a movie as regularly as possible. Avoid causing suffering for the rest of the family as a way to comfort the suffering child. If as parents we are positive about the situation, children are resilient and cope easily. This also helps the other children have genuine care for their struggling sibling instead of developing resentment.

Communication should be emphasized to allow children to express themselves always, because home routines can be interrupted easily whenever there is a child with advanced needs in a family. This may be normal life in such a family, but it really is not the norm. It is tedious, and many things can fall through cracks if attention is not intentionally maintained for all children's needs. The children without advanced needs can easily feel overlooked and even unloved because they don't understand the energy involved to take care of their sibling. Communicating love and care regularly and checking in on the other children's emotional needs regularly is necessary.

Never expect your other children to understand the situation, especially at a young age, because they won't understand. They are children and deserve your care, and lack of it will affect them negatively even into adulthood. This can also affect your relationship with your children forever.

Be intentional about paying attention to your other children, spending uninterrupted time with them, and playing games together. Some children develop Psychological sickness and habits as a mean to demand attention which can affect their life as they get old. Children should never be expected to understand how difficult the situation may be. They may express disappointment and even frustration when they are not given attention which can develop into other complications if not attended to. Purpose to give attention to all your children so that they are not demanding it in unhealthy ways. This might mean having others watch your child with advanced needs some of the time to be able to give adequate time to your other children's needs. It pays off for everyone with intention. How we deal with the situation can affect all relationships in the family positively or negatively long term. Because we want good relationships, we need to seek out ways to create those lasting, healthy, and strong relationships that last a lifetime with all our children and between our children as they grow into adults.

As the Parent/Guardian Caregiver

Generally, the life of a caregiver is extremely difficult. It is easy to drown in the roughness of life that comes with raising a child with an unusual condition, and it is necessary to find ways to cope. Think about it; many parents in this parenting situation can hardly plan their days because they are regularly dealing with emergencies and unplanned situations due to their child with advanced needs. There can be regular sleepless nights and constant demands. The emotional pain and dilemma involved is huge, and in some situations, trauma is added to it. This may not have the same effect on all parents, but being intentional about parenting in such a situation can help reduce negative effect. Following are some examples of things that can be helpful include.

Having an Inner Awareness Is Helpful

This is one of the most precious of things to develop in life, especially when faced with regular difficult situations. Self-awareness is having a conscious concept of who you are on the inside. It includes coming to terms with your personality, strengths, weaknesses, beliefs, motivation, thoughts, and emotions/feelings. Practicing self-awareness allows you to see where your thoughts and emotions are taking you, which helps you control your behavior, which, in turn, helps shape your character. Self-awareness also helps you make the changes in your life that you want to make. Being aware in the moment of what you are feeling or thinking helps you control your behavior instead of leading you to act without thinking. Being self-aware makes it easier for you to understand how others perceive you. It helps you relate better and be received better by others. It is one of the attributes of emotional intelligence that helps you succeed in controlling your emotions. The more you develop self-awareness, the more you can accept yourself as an individual who is separate from your environment and from others around you. It helps you develop your own worth as a person, refining what you hope for in life. It also helps in interpreting the situation surrounding us better.

Going through the process of learning how self-awareness works not only helps build other relationships, but also help greatly in your personal life, especially as a caregiver. It helps bring ease to admitting our emotions and our thought processes. Being aware of what is cooking inside us can help us pay attention to how what we feel affects our environment and our responses. When we understand ourselves, we can express to others what we are feeling and what our needs are. It makes it easier to be a parent because we can easily be okay with just being. Even in times when we feel like God has deserted us, we can accept that this is how we are feeling. We are more comfortable to express to others how we feel or what we are thinking, and they can pray for us. Many undesirable emotions and thoughts can come with being a caregiver. This is normal, and it is health to give ourselves permission to be real.

Taking time to understand ourselves helps us come to terms with what we want in life. It also helps in choosing the people we spend the most time with. As caregivers, we must realize that it is critical to take care of ourselves. The circumstances leave you with less to live on than people whose lives are stable have. People can also mean well but be very hurtful for parents in this situation by what they say or how they act. Sometimes, you might share things because you need to talk, but those you share with might be ready with answers for you and feel disappointed that you are not following their advice. There aren't many listeners. Being aware of how people make you feel is helpful in building your boundaries as a caregiver.

Self-Educating

"My people are destroyed for lack of knowledge; because you have rejected knowledge, I reject you from being a priest to me. And since you have forgotten the law of your God, I also will forget your children" (Hosea 4:6 ESV).

As the saying goes, knowledge is power. The more you know about anything, the better it is for you. Raising a child with advanced needs is difficult, but the more you understand your child's condition, medications, and whatever is available for the situation, the better decisions you can make for yourself, your children, and other members of the family. It helps you advocate for your child when you better understand what you are dealing with. It also helps you find programs that are helpful for your child's treatment and well-being.

Many good doctors give caregivers and patients a chance to

express what they are looking for, but when a patient or caregiver doesn't know what he or she wants or what the diagnosis means, doctors are forced to make decisions based on their judgment of the person they're trying to help. Along with self-educating, the more you know your child and his or her potential, the more you can work with the medical team to bring the best out of your child instead of putting your child into a treatment class. For example, children with seizures may be expected to act a certain way. A generalized plan of action can be put in place for children who suffer seizure, but that plan may not be appropriate for your child. It takes more work to know your child well under some circumstances and to understand his or her condition, but it is beneficial to the child when you take the time and learn as much as you can.

Likewise, studying the scriptures and understanding what God says about your situation as a caregiver and about your child helps know how to pray effectively. Praying the word catches the attention of God, because He promises that his word does not return to Him void but accomplishes what it is meant to. Some things don't make sense, but following God's words brings the outcome that doesn't make sense, because it doesn't come the natural way but the supernatural way by God's power. Miracles still happen, and God is still at work, but we must learn to apply His word to our circumstances.

A Practice of Spiritual Alertness

Deliberately being aware of God's presence our lives is helpful. This means to look for the ways in which God is working our lives each day. There is a secret in Proverbs 3:6 (NKJV): "In all your ways acknowledge Him, And He shall direct your paths." It helps to sit back each day and reflect on the day, being thankful to God. We didn't live through the day because we planned to, but it is by God's grace. In advanced parenting, it might be difficult to plan, depending on the situation you are dealing with. Learning to keep your spiritual ears attentive to God's guidance brings sanity during difficult times, because He is never wrong, even when we don't understand. The Holy Spirit knows all things pertaining to us and our circumstances and guides us when we learn to depend on Him.

Engaging in Spiritual Warfare

Whether you are aware of this or not, life is full of warfare. Being aware of this and paying attention to your heart helps in many ways. Because we are spiritual beings living in human bodies, our warfare is spiritual in nature. It only sometimes manifests in the physical realm. The Spirit of God warns us when something is about to happen and helps us in our weaknesses. The things that happen in our children's lives and in our lives, are not always the will of God and have no purpose other than the enemy attacking to stop us from fulfilling our purpose. We live in a fallen world, and warfare will be part of our lives until Christ comes back. We should therefore be intentional about our prayer lives and battle against the enemy. We should learn to pay attention to our hearts, to stop when prompted to stop, and to move when prompted to move. Warfare is part of living in a fallen world, and we must always be ready. We fight our battles on our knees. Ephesians 6:10 tells us that our war is not against flesh and blood but that it is spiritual. No matter how warfare comes to us, it is important to keep in mind that God's kingdom is under attack and it is not about us. Matthew 11:12 (NASB) says, "From the days of John the Baptist until now the kingdom of heaven suffers violence, and violent men take it by force."

Developing Resilience

"God is our refuge and strength, A very present help in trouble. Therefore we will not fear, Even though the earth be removed, And though the mountains be carried into the midst of the sea; Though its waters roar and be troubled, Though the mountains shake with its swelling" (Psalm 46:1–3 NKJV).

Raising a child with advanced needs is difficult, and the things you deal with can be tough and traumatizing. Resilience is the ability to face difficult life situations—for example, trauma, sickness, or divorce—and bounce back without being altered greatly. It is the ability to bear or to recover successfully from difficult conditions. Some people have more resilience than others, but the good news is that resilience can be developed by any person who is willing to work at it. I believe that resilience begins with the realization that life is not easy but that all things are possible. Second, I believe that God is more powerful than anything life or death may bring my way. Giving Him control brings us peace in difficult situations. Life will always present challenges. It helps to develop a positive way of overcoming life's difficulties. Instead of focusing on the mountains ahead of you, learn to focus on the Creator of the heaven and the earth and on His ability to move any mountain that stands in the way or to raise you above the mountains. Listening to other people's stories encourages us, because we are not alone in the suffering. If others are moving forward, we can move forward too.

Develop in Discernment

Have you ever entered a home and right away felt that something was different, only to find out later there had been a fight before you arrived? Have you ever met someone and felt great about that person only to find out that he or she was a wonderful person? Have you ever been in a house and sensed that something was not right, only to find out later that the house caught on fire after you left? All these things are signs of God's spirit in our hearts. Discernment is God revealing things of the spirit to you before it is made clear in the natural.

Discernment in Christian contexts is perception in the absence of judgment, which helps a person obtain spiritual direction and understanding. It is the ability to understand spiritual truth. According to the Bible, we are required to test all things: "But test everything; hold fast what is good. Abstain from every form of evil" (1 Thessalonians 5:21–22 ESV). "Beloved, do not believe every spirit, but test the spirits to see whether they are from God, for many false prophets have gone out into the world" (1 John 4:1 ESV).

The ability to test things and to see them from God's point of view is what is known as discernment. Discernment, as mentioned earlier, gives you the ability to see accurately what is not evident to many people around you.

Spiritual discernment is not meant only for some people; it is available to all believers. Discernment is a prerequisite of wisdom and is to be desired by all believers. No one can have spiritual discernment without God. When raising a child with advanced needs, discernment can lead you to the right doctors and other medical places and to the right environment for your child and for yourself to maintain healthy spiritual and emotional state.

Learn to Encourage Yourself

"Be strong and take heart, all you who hope in the Lord" (Psalm 31:24 NKJV).

There comes a time in life when you realize that life is busy and that the people in your life have their own lives. They have their problems and their joys. Sometimes your sorrows get in the way of the people whom you love and who love you. That is life.

While it is wonderful to have people in your life, there will be times those closest to you cannot identify with your pain, let alone those who don't care about you. Other people care and want to support you but don't know how or are not able when you need them the most. Other times, those close to you may be in need at the same time you need them.

> Then Jesus went with them to a place called Gethsemane, and he said to his disciples, "Sit here, while I go over there and pray." And taking with him Peter and the two sons of Zebedee, he began to be sorrowful and troubled. Then he said to them, "My soul is very sorrowful, even to death; remain here, and watch with me." And going a little farther he fell on his face and prayed, saying, "My Father, if it be possible, let this cup pass from me; nevertheless, not as I will, but as you will." And he came to the disciples and found them sleeping. And he said to Peter, "So, could you not watch with me one hour? Watch and pray that you may not enter into temptation. The spirit indeed is willing, but the flesh is weak." Again, for the second time, he went away and prayed, "My Father, if this cannot pass unless I drink it, your will be done." And again, he came and found them sleeping, for their eyes were heavy. So, leaving them again, he went away and prayed for the third time, saying the same words again. Then he came to the disciples and said to them, "Sleep and take your rest later on. See, the hour is at hand, and the Son of Man is betrayed into the hands of sinners. Rise, let us be going; see, my betrayer is at hand." Matthew 26:36-44 NKJV.

Sometimes people will judge you and make your life miserable when you need support the most. Fortunately, this is found to happen throughout the Bible.

First Samuel 30:6 (NKJV) is a good a good example: "And David was greatly distressed; for the people spoke of stoning him, because the soul of all the people was grieved, every man for his sons and for his daughters: but David encouraged himself in the Lord his God."

People are entitled to their opinions, and we can't do anything about what they choose as their opinions. But their opinions do not have the power to make you or break you unless you allow it. The only opinion that has power over you is your opinion of yourself. We must learn to pick our pieces and encourage ourselves in the Lord, because many times in life, we will need to encourage ourselves no matter how great we have it. Jesus went through it, and even his disciples denied him and betrayed him. He had to encourage Himself. Fortunately, we have Him to help us in those lonely times of our lives in advanced parenting and other tough life situations.

Forgiving Is Necessary

Holding onto unforgiveness keeps us captive. When we forgive someone for doing us wrong, we set ourselves free to move forward with our lives. Holding onto unforgiveness may not affect the person who hurt you, but it will have a negative effect on you. The longer you hold onto it, the more it will affect you negatively and drain you of energy. Forgiveness can take different forms depending on the violation, but keep in mind the effect it will have on you helps you find the will to do it.

When we are raising a child with advanced needs, we have more opportunities for people to hurt us more than usual, because we are dealing with a sensitive situation. Learning to forgive is part of taking care of ourselves to give our best to our loved ones. We also must learn to receive forgiveness when we do wrong. God wants us to receive His gift of grace like our little children receive gifts from us parents. God did it all for us, and with His help, we ought to forgive ourselves and forgive others for our own sake at least.

Forgiving also keeps blessings flowing into your life because it keeps your path to God clear when you pray.

Being Okay with Personal Boundaries

A boundary is a mark that shows an area's outermost limits. It is necessary to have boundaries to mark our limits. Personal boundaries are guidelines that you come up with to keep yourself safe—for example, having a limit on how others may behave toward you. Boundaries are usually built out of spiritual beliefs, cultural beliefs, past experiences, people's opinions, and the like. Because life is not fair and because not everyone thinks as you do, you must develop limits to guide your relationships. It is okay to say no and not feel guilty about it or have a need to explain yourself. For example, almost every preacher on television asks for financial support. How much can one person give to all the preachers on television? It is their job to ask for support because they need the support, and it is your job to discern who to give to and who not to give to because you can't give to everyone asking even if you wanted to. Jesus exercised strong boundaries and did not apologize to anyone about it, which should give believers permission to do likewise for our sanity and health. When doing advance parenting, we have a greater reason to exercise stronger boundaries, because while many mean well, things can be more draining to a parent under such circumstances.

Family and Other Important Relationships

Having family and friends who truly care about you can be very helpful in coping with advanced parenting. I don't believe that any person is able to get through life alone. We must be wise in choosing relationships that support us and that we can trust to support us through tough times. We also must discern which relationships are damaging for us when we have a tough situation to deal with. Unfortunately, bad relationships can be very time-consuming and take a lot of energy, which you don't have much of in advanced parenting. We need good relationships, and we need to avoid those relationships that drain and waste our time and energy.

Moments of Solitude

As wonderful as it is to have people who love you around, it is beneficial to practice solitude to give God time for inner work and healing.

Solitude gives us a place to do a self-evaluation on our true emotions, thought lives, and other things of importance (like our children). Intentional moments of solitude force us to pay attention to how our business is affecting our health and our eating patterns and why. That helps us to deal with most problems sooner rather than later. Moments of solitude also will give you a comfortable place to do some of the things that are not comfortable to do with other people around, for example, making out confessions to counter negative thoughts or emotions, crying if necessary without being asked why you are crying, or just being.

Exercise, Nutrition, and General Health

It takes discipline to live a healthy life. Practicing discipline leads to a healthy lifestyle. As a parent with a child that has advanced needs, it is vital to take care of your health, which includes what you eat, sleep, and drink and how often you exercise. The better health you maintain, the more you will have to give to your family. Taking care of your health shows you care for your loved ones. The food we eat makes a difference in how we feel, and exercise helps us sleep better and feel better, in addition to the many other benefits it has for our mental and physical health.

Journaling

When raising a child with advanced needs, journaling helps keep life easier and simpler, because you don't need to remember everything since you write it down. It helps keep track of events, effects of medications, and other treatments, which can be vital in finding proper treatment for your child. It keeps the facts as facts. It is one thing to try to recall what happened in a certain situation and another thing to know what happened because you wrote it down as it happened. Journaling can help you advocate for your child, because it makes it easier to follow the results of treatments. Written facts are very helpful in many occasions. When they aren't helpful, you can have peace in having done your best.

Journaling is also therapeutic for many people. It helps with processing our emotions and thoughts. Many times, you are not ready to talk about something, writing it down can help bring peace of mind and even find some solutions within you heart. Once something is written, it can lead to more questions which sometimes will lead you to study more about your situation. Journaling can keep you from feeling overwhelmed.

Decide Never to Quit

"Life is tough, and only the tough make it." That is a statement that has lived long. It is understandable that some individuals end up with life conditions that limit them in terms of what they can achieve. Yet even some of the limited people do much better in life than many who have fewer limitations. Life can be challenging for some people, especially parents with a child who is medically challenged or has disabilities. Every parent hopes for the best for their children, including children with advanced needs. Carrying the emotions involved in continuously dealing with a tough situation can be very challenging, and some can make a parent wearily. The decision to never quit helps get through those time that are easy to quit. With great determination, many situation concerning our children can be turned around for good, which is a great reason to never quit.

PART 5

Conclusion

E very parent's desire is to have successful children and maintain good relationships with their children all their lives. In fact, this desire ends up being the very hindrance for the great relationships we all hope for as parents. On the day your baby comes home, there is great excitement, joy, and laughter. No parent at that moment foresees anything going wrong in the life of that baby or having a rough relationship with him or her. However, as time goes and the child starts to grow, things begin to change. Sometimes, the expectations of a parent are so frustrating that it is shocking. Sometimes, it turns to constant tears and pain. Old age comes many times, and children are not involved at all. What happens?

Our children have minds of their own. From the moment, you bring that bundle of joy into your life, keep in mind he or she is not a mini you in person. You have a full person in your life in the form of a baby. You don't know your children just because you gave birth to them. It will take having a relationship to know who you brought into your life like any other person you meet. This can be starting point into working on your relationship with your children. Focus on building them into whole, good, productive, healthy people instead of focusing on your needs as the parent. Do what is right for your children, and you will not have to worry about making them love you. They will not only love you, but also be very thankful to you forever once their lives turn out right due to your efforts for them.

Start by understanding yourself first. Understanding where you are in your journey and what your needs are is not about being perfect, because no one is perfect. It is about working at developing yourself to have more to give to your children. Take time to understand what kind of a relationship you have with yourself. How you view yourself will determine how you will view your children and others in your life, which has the potential to affect your relationships. Keep in mind that we can only give what we have. If we are running on negative, we may have the right intention but never be able to act on it, which leaves us guilt-ridden and feeling worse about ourselves and being worse at what we hope to get better at.

Understand how you parent and the effects of your parenting style. There are four recognized parenting styles according to psychology, and it helps to understand each style to gauge where you are and what changes you can make to improve on your parenting. The next step is to become intentional about your choices. Good relationships take time and effort. They don't just happen. Likewise, with our children, we must become intentional and not take it for granted that they will always be crazy in love with us because we are their parents.

The end results of focusing in raising our children in wholeness is adults who are whole, and having strong, lifelong relationship with them is part of the package. The wholeness of a person determines his or her success in all aspects of life, including relationships. Contentment of the heart is not brought about by fame, wealth, people, or poverty like some people believe or other external things. Contentment is a state of the heart that is caused by the wholeness of a person. This means that a person finds fulfillment from within, not from outward sources. This is an important reason we need to focus on the wholeness of our children while we are raising them. We should help them be happy with who they are without any external things added to them. Building them into solid people helps them handle life better in plenty and in little, in tough times and in good times, etc.

Mistakes can happen when a child's identity is confused with outward success. Outward things can change and do often change, but who we are does not change. It is important for children to understand that who they are is not based on their achievements. Who they are is who God says they are, and that is solid. We need to help our children understand that external things might make us happy, but they do not define or fulfill us. Help them deal well with disappointments while they are young, because life is full of disappointments. Instead of shielding their feelings from getting hurt by keeping them from health competitions, sports, and music, expose them to such things and help them deal with disappointment. Winning or not winning in competition doesn't change their identities. They are still special and precious. Help them understand that circumstances change in life, but who they are within does not change.

Basically, parenting is a tough job, especially for parents that are working at being intentional. However, it comes with great joys and can be very rewarding all lifelong. It ultimately brings God glory when our children maximize their potential and maintain healthy, loving relationships with their parents and others in life. Every child is a gift from God and should be raised in fear of God. Commit each child to the Lord for His purpose.

"Behold, children *are* a heritage from the LORD, the fruit of the womb *is* a reward. ⁴ Like arrows in the hand of a warrior, so *are* the children of one's youth. ⁵ Happy *is* the man who has his quiver full of them" (Psalm 127:3–5 NKJV).

ABOUT THE AUTHOR

(SUMMARY).

Ann Makena is a wife and a mother. She is an author of other inspirational books. Ann is an independent instructor through community education. She is a co-host of a local TV show. She is an ordained minister and bible teacher. She is the founder of sister charitable organizations in U.S. and in Kenya.

Ann previously served as a full-time hospice chaplain for 10 years. She also volunteered for a Christian counseling crisis center for 4 years. Ann has a M.A in Ministry leadership, M.A in Theological studies, B.S. in Psychology-Counseling, and B.A. in Divinity. She also went through C.P.E. (Clinical Pastoral Education).

(IN DEPTH).

Ann Makena is a wife and a mother. She is the author of books including, "Parenting into Wholeness", "Become Whole, Unbreakable and Unstoppable" and "Knowing and Yielding to The Voice That Counts" She is the co-author of "Miracles Still Happen, IF YOU DON'T BELIEVE-EXPLAIN ME" with her son Nate (who was not expected to survive at birth and has endured major medical complications but is thriving). Her daughter Sally who was born about 2lbs is healthy, thriving academically, enjoys poetry, and music among other things. Ann has been a single mother who has raised her child with severe medical conditions and she has found great success. She is also a great advocate for strong, healthy, and happy marriages with her husband Steve. Ann is an independent instructor through community education who offers classes on parenting, diversity and intercultural subjects, personal growth, and other subjects. She is a co-host of a local TV show within Twin Cities metro area. She is an ordained minister and a bible teacher. She is the founder of sister charitable organizations in U.S. and in Kenya which are providing home and advocating for orphaned and abandoned children, ministering to single mothers, victims and survivors of domestic violence, oppressed girls, and women among other ministries. To learn more visit www. citysheartcryministries. org. Ann previously served as a full-time hospice chaplain for 10 years. Her experience includes spiritual and emotional support for patients and their families, officiating funerals, and other services. She also volunteered for a Christian counseling crisis center once a week for 4 years. Ann has a M.A in Ministry leadership, M.A in Theological studies, B.S. in Psychology-Counseling, and B.A. in Divinity. She also went through C.P.E. (Clinical Pastoral Education). Ann's favorite scripture is; "Trust in the LORD with all your heart, and lean not on your own understanding; In all your ways acknowledge Him, And He shall direct your paths," (Proverbs 3:5-6 NKJV).

Ann Makena as a mother

I am the mother of Nate Munene and Sally Makena. Nate was not expected to survive at birth. He did not only survive but is a thriving teenager. Although he has endured a tough medical journey including about 20 brain surgeries, severe battle with seizures, numerous hospitalization etc., he has no self-pity. He has a positive attitude, is a hard worker, is loving and looks out for others, and is the main author of "Miracles Still Happen" IF YOU DON'T BELIEVE-EXPLAIN ME. He is growing into an inspirational speaker encouraging others not to give up in spite of life struggles. Sally was about 2lbs at birth. She is compassionate, hard-working and likes to help others. Sally at the age of 6 competed at national level in poetry representing the state of Minnesota at NAM. Steve and I put the peace and happiness of our home first and open to others in times of need. The principles I am sharing in this book are working for me and I believe they will work for you if you apply them. I also encourage you to develop more principles of your own. There is no limit to learning and growing. God, bless you.

CPSIA information can be obtained
at www.ICGtesting.com
Printed in the USA
FFOW03n1709121117
43468744-42141FF